Kirsty Dunseath was born and grew up in Bangor, Northern Ireland. She studied French and Spanish at St Andrews University before moving to London. She has worked as an editor for several years, and is currently employed at The Women's Press.

A Second Skin

WOMEN WRITE ABOUT CLOTHES

Kirsty Dunseath, editor

First published by The Women's Press Ltd, 1998
A member of the Namara Group
34 Great Sutton Street, London EC1V 0DX

British Library Cataloguing-in-Publication Data
A catalogue record for this book is available from the British Library.

ISBN 0 7043 4588 9

Typeset in Bembo 11/13pt by FSH Ltd, London
Printed and bound in Great Britain by Cox & Wyman Ltd,
Reading, Berkshire

Contents

Introduction

'Clothes never remain a question of pure aesthetics; far too much personal feeling is involved in them. They play such an important part in the delicate business of getting oneself across that it seems impossible to discuss them, for long, objectively,' wrote Elizabeth Bowen in 1950.[1] The sumptuous array of pieces written for this anthology is testimony to that fact. Witty, moving, shocking, political and sensual, these pieces are anything but dispassionate.

Some would argue that clothes are just 'things'; that they are frivolous, trivial products of the fashion industry. And they can be sheer good fun and a source of great pleasure. But we live in a world filled with inanimate objects which form an intrinsic part of our lives and to which we often assign meaning or significance. From the earliest times, humans have chosen to mark or adorn the body for specific purposes and what clearer adornment do we have than what we choose to put on each day?

From the pieces of writing included in *A Second Skin*, it is clear that clothes very much form a part of and reflect our sense of self, whether it be consciously or subconsciously. They are not just about enveloping the body – they connect with memory, identity, history, ritual, culture, race, sexuality and

---

1 Elizabeth Bowen, *Collected Impressions*, Longmans, Green & Co., 1950

sensuality. They are about how we relate the realm of subjective experience to the objective world around us.

The women in this collection revel in the texture of cloth and the vivid associations of colour. The clothes they have chosen to 'stain with words and stories' (Margaret Atwood), speak of themes such as love, death, adolescence, friendship and motherhood. Carol Shields and Caryn Franklin describe particular items which marked their rite of passage into adulthood; A L Kennedy and bell hooks explore the connection between clothes and sexuality; Joan Smith and Sarah Dreher look at the politics of what we wear; Jean Buffong and Manju Kak discuss the cultural resonances of clothing; Catherine Dunne and Andrea Stuart show how clothes interrelate with history; and Margaret Atwood, Janice Galloway and Joyce Carol Oates examine the way clothes can reflect the complex relationship between a mother and a daughter.

From silver shoes to stripy socks, from purple crimplene to luxurious cashmere, these pieces bear witness to the fascinating diversity of women's experience and the rich fabric of our lives.

I would like to thank all the contributors for their enthusiasm and support and also Githa Hariharan who suggested the idea of publishing an anthology on clothes.

Kirsty Dunseath

A Second Skin

The Scarf
Joyce Carol Oates

A turquoise silk scarf, elegantly long, and narrow; so delicately threaded with pale gold and silver butterflies, you might lose yourself in a dream contemplating it, imagining you're gazing into another dimension or another time in which the heraldic butterflies are living creatures with slow, pulsing wings.

Eleven years old, I was searching for a birthday present for my mother. *Mom* she was to me, though often in weak moments I'd hear my voice cry *Mommy*.

It was a windy grit-borne Saturday in late March, a week before Easter, and cold. Searching through the stores of downtown Strykersville. Not Woolworth's, not Rexall's Drugs, not Norban's Discounts where a gang of girls might prowl after school but the 'better' women's stores where few of us went except with our mothers, and rarely even then.

Saved jealously, in secret, for many months in a bunched-up white sock in my bureau drawer was eight dollars and sixty-five cents; in my jacket pocket, the bills carefully folded. This sum was sufficient, I believed, for a really nice, really special present for my mother. I was excited, nervous; already I could see the surprised pleasure in my mother's eyes as she unwrapped the box, and this was to be my reward. For there was a delicious way Mom had of squinching up her face, which was an unlined, pretty face, a young-woman face still, and saying, in her warm whispery voice, as if this were a secret between us, 'Oh, honey, what have you *done* – !'

I wanted to strike that match bringing out the warm startled glow in my mother's face, that glisten in her eyes.

I wanted to present my mother with, not a mere store-bought item, but a love-offering. A talisman against harm. The perfect gift that would be a spell against hurt, fear, aloneness; sorrow, illness, age and death and oblivion. The gift that would say *I love, you are life to me.*

Had I eighteen dollars, or eighty, I would have wished to spend every penny on this gift for my mother's birthday. To hand over every penny I'd saved, to make the transaction sacred. For I believed that this secretly hoarded money had to be surrendered to the proper authority for the transaction to be valid, sacred; and this mysterious authority resided in one of the 'better' stores and nowhere else. So there was a heat, a feverish glare in my eyes and an eager, awkward motion to my slight body as if, even as I lunged forward, I was yet bracing myself, steeling myself, in a kind of physical chagrin.

Naturally, I aroused suspicion in the primly well-dressed women who clerked in such stores. The better-dressed the salesclerk, the more immediate her suspicion. There were several stores experienced in such a nightmare haze of blindness and breathlessness, I was inside, and out, in a matter of seconds before even quite hearing the sharp query meant to intimidate and expel – 'Yes? May I assist you?'

At last I found myself amid glittery glass display cases and racks of beautiful leather goods hanging like the slain carcasses of animals. A well-worn parquet floor creaked incriminatingly beneath my feet. How had I dared enter Kenilworth's Ladies Fashions where mother never shopped? What gusty wind had propelled me inside, like a taunting hand on the flat of my back? The lady salesclerk, tight-corseted with a scratchy steel-wool bun at the nape of he neck and smacking-red downturned mouth, eyed my every movement up and down the dazzling aisles. 'May I assist you, miss?' this lady asked in a cold, doubtful voice. I murmured I was just looking. 'Did you come to look, miss, or to buy?' My face pounded with blood as if I'd been turned upside-down. This woman didn't trust me! At school I was such a good girl; such a diligent student; always an A-student; always a favorite of teachers; one of those students who is on a teacher's side in the fray, thus not to be despised. But here in Kenilworth's, it seemed, I was not to be trusted. I might have been a little black girl for my dark hair was suspiciously curly-kinky like moist wires, and inclined to frizz like something demented. You would know, seeing me, that such a specimen could not drag a decent comb through that head of snarly hair. And my skin was olive-dark, not the wholesome buttermilk-pale, like the salesclerk's powdered skin, that was preferred. Here was a poor girl, an ungainly girl, a shy girl; therefore a dishonest girl, a sneaky little shoplifter, just give her the chance, just turn your back for an instant.

It was my ill luck that no other customers were in this department of Kenilworth's at that moment and so the clerk could fiercely concentrate all her attention on me. How prized I was, not requiring the usual courtesy and fawning-over with which you must serve a true customer. For I was not a 'customer', but an intruder, a trespasser. *She expects me to steal* – the thought rushed at me with the force of a radio news bulletin. What hurt and resentment I felt, what shame. Yet, how badly I would have liked, at that moment, to steal; to slip something, oh anything! into my pocket – a leather wallet, a small beaded handbag, a lacy white Irish linen handkerchief. But I dared not, for I was a 'good' girl who never, in the company of my gang of friends, purloined even cheap plastic lipsticks, fake-gold hair barrettes and key rings adorned with the ecstatic smiling faces of Jane Russell, Linda Darnell, Debra Paget and Lana Turner. So I stood paralyzed in the gaze of the woman sales clerk; *she wants me to steal but I can't, I won't.*

In a weak voice I said, 'It's for my mother – a birthday present. How much is – this?' I'd been staring at a display of scarfs. The price tags on certain of the items of merchandise – the wallets, the handbags, even gloves and handkerchiefs – were so absurdly high, my eye took them in even as my brain repelled them; information-bits not to be assimilated. Scarfs, I seemed to believe, would be more reasonably priced. And what beautiful scarfs were on display – I stared almost without comprehension at these lovely colors, these exquisite fabrics and designs. For these were not coarse, practical, cotton-flannel scarfs like the kind I wore most of the winter, that tied tightly beneath the chin; scarfs that kept one's hair from whipping into snarls, kept ears and neck warm; scarfs that looked, at their frequent worst, not unlike bandages wrapped around the head. These scarfs were works of art. They were made of fine silk, or very light wool; they were extravagantly long, or triangular; some were squares; some were enormous, with fringes – perhaps these were shawls. There were paisley prints, there were floral prints. There were gossamer scarfs, gauzy scarfs, scarfs boldly printed with yellow jonquils and luscious red tulips, scarfs wispy as those dreams of surpassing sweetness that, as we wake and yearn to draw them after us, break and disintegrate like strands of cobweb. Blindly I pointed at – I didn't dare touch – the most beautiful of the scarfs, turquoise, a fine delicate silk patterned with small gold and silver figures I couldn't quite decipher. Through her pinched-looking bifocals the salesclerk peered at me, saying, in a voice of reproach, '*That* scarf is pure silk, from China. *That* scarf is – ', pausing then to consider me as if for the first time. Maybe she felt in the air the tremor and heat of my blood. Maybe it was simple pity. This utterly mysterious transaction, one of those unfathomable and incalculable events that mark at rare intervals the inner curve of our lives, gratuitious moments of grace. In a lowered, more kindly voice, though with an edge of adult annoyance, the salesclerk said, 'It's ten dollars. Plus tax.'

Ten dollars. I began numbly to remove my savings from my pocket, six wrinkled dollars and nickels, dimes, a single quarter and numerous pennies, counting them with frowning earnestness as if I hadn't any idea what they might add up to. The sharp-eyed salesclerk said irritably, ' – I mean eight dollars. It's been marked down to eight dollars for our Easter sale.' Eight dollars! I said, stammering, 'I – I'll take it. Thank you.' Relief so flooded me I might have fainted. I was smiling, triumphant. I couldn't believe my good luck even as, with childish egotism, I never paused to doubt it.

Mother insists *But I have no more use for this, dear. Please take it.* Rummaging through closets, bureau drawers of the old house soon to be sold to strangers. In her calm melodic voice that belies the shakiness of her hands saying *If – later – something happens to me – I don't want it to be lost.*

Each visit back home, Mother has more to give me. Things once precious out of the ever-more remote, receding past. What is the secret meaning of such gift-giving by a woman of eighty-three, don't inquire.

Mother speaks often, vaguely, of *lost*. She fears papers being lost – insurance policies, medical records. *Lost* is a bottomless ravine into which you might fall, and fall. Into which her several sisters and brothers have disappeared one by one, and a number of her friends. And Father – has it already been a year? So that, for the remainder of her life – Mother's life grown mysterious to her as a dream that continues ceaselessly without defining itself, without the rude interruption of lucidity – she will wake in the morning wondering where has Dad gone? She reaches out and there's no one beside her so she tells herself, He's in the bathroom. And, almost, she can hear him in there. Later she thinks, He must be outside. And, almost, she can hear the lawnmower. Or she thinks, He's taken the car. And gone – where?

'Here! Here it is.'

At the bottom of a drawer in a bedroom bureau Mother has found what she's been searching for with such concentration. This afternoon she has pressed upon me a square-cut amethyst in an antique setting, a ring once belonging to her mother-in-law, and a handwoven potholder only just perceptibly marred by scorch. And now she opens a long flat box, and there it is, amid tissue paper: the silk turquoise scarf with its pale heraldic butterflies.

For a moment, I can't speak. I've gone entirely numb.

Fifty years. Can it have been – fifty years.

Says Mother, proudly, 'Your father gave it to me. When we were just married. It was my favorite scarf but you can see – it was too pretty to wear, and too thin. So I put it away.'

'But you did wear it, Mother. I remember.'

'Did I?' – that look of veiled, just perceptible annoyance. She doesn't wish to be corrected. Saying, 'Please take it, dear. It would make me happy if you did.'

'But – '

'I don't have any use for it, and I don't want it to get *lost*.'

I lift the turquoise scarf from the box, staring. Admiring. In fact its label is French, not Chinese. In fact the turquoise isn't as vivid as I would have remembered. Fifty years ago, on what would have been her thirty-third birthday, my mother had opened her present with an odd air of anxiety; the luxuriant wrapping, the embossed silver KENILWORTH's on the box must have alarmed her. Taking the scarf from the box she'd been speechless for a long moment before saying, 'Why, honey – it's *beautiful*. How did you – ' Her voice, usually so confident, trailed off. As if words failed her. Or, with her subtle sense to tact, she believed it would be rude to make such an inquiry even of an eleven-year-old daughter.

That talisman that says *I love you. You are life to me.*

This luminous silky scarf imprinted with butterflies like ancient heraldic coins. It's the kind of imported, expensive scarf stylish women are wearing today, flung casually over their shoulders. I ask my mother if she's certain she wants to give away the scarf though I know the answer: for Mother has come to an age when she knows exactly what she wants and what she doesn't want, what she needs and doesn't need. Saying yes she's certain, arranging the scarf around my neck, tying the ends, untying the ends, frowning beside me at the mirror.

'See, darling? It's beautiful on *you.*'

My Beautiful Brothel Creepers
Deborah Levy

When I was seventeen and bought my first pair of brothel creepers from Shellys, I knew they would never be worn with socks. It has always been very clear to me that men and women who wear shoes without socks are destined to become my friends and lovers. These sockless people have a kind of abandon and suppleness in their body. They walk with zip. At the same time they manage to look both nonchalant and excitable. To not wear socks is to be alert, but not hearty. To not wear socks is to not pretend that love is for ever.

Five months pregnant and wearing my brothel creepers, I went to see a Peter Greenaway film called *The Baby of Mâcon*. The best moment was when a counter-tenor started to sing something that sounded like *the fluids of the body. . . love passeth quickly*. These seemed such beautiful words to sum up everything that matters in life that I cried and cried until my white shirt was sopping wet with my own salty fluids.

Love does pass quickly and there is no time to waste putting on socks. To wear socks with your shoes is to have missed your date with love. If it's any consolation, people who wear socks are probably better adjusted than their sockless brothers and sisters. They are not in weather denial, they face up to things and always carry an umbrella when it rains.

They also fear sex and sensuality (particularly those who wear sandals *and* socks), and are terrified of revealing they are in fact libido-crazed sado-masochistic authoritarians pretending to be bird watchers and vegetarians.

The sockless are Godless. So are brothel creepers, also known as 'teddy boy shoes'. Walking down the street in my very first pair made me feel like I was wearing a tattoo that marked me out for a meaningful life. Not quite winkle pickers, their leopardskin tongue (V shaped) was surrounded by two inches of thick black crepe sole. To slip my naked foot into them was to literally walk on air. My brothel creepers were beauty and truth, genius personified, never mind they were rock and bop – that was not the point. They were the metropolis, my ticket out of suburbia, my exit sign from everything women were supposed to become.

There was something in the brothel creeper design that seemed to put the world in perspective. The combination of brothel creeper and naked ankles made me feel sexy, serious, frivolous, confident. I wore them with tight black clinging dresses and I wore them with jeans. I wore them with pencil skirts and pin-striped trousers. I was never not wearing them ever. Their pointy black toes tapped to the beat of rebellion; the shoes my mother would never have worn, the shoes my father would never have worn, in fact the shoes not many girls wore but the ones who did were always gorgeous. My narcissism was confirmed when, hungry, I found myself waiting on the platform of a station somewhere in the sleepy shires. When I heard the train was going to be eleven minutes late, I sprinted over the bridge (in my beautiful brothel creepers) to find something to eat. Everyone in the local supermarket was olde and if they weren't pensioners they were younge. I grabbed a sandwich and ran to the checkout till, four minutes to go before my train arrived. And there was the checkout girl in her checkout overalls staring dreamily into the white strobes on the ceiling. Three minutes to go and her till roll runs out. As she stands up to get another one, I see she is wearing brothel creepers too. Except hers are electric blue suede and have even more attitude than my own. As I run for my train I know that she too will run out of her till roll life one day, because her shoes are a sign that she has hope. HOPE! After the revolution every one will have a pair.

I have bought many versions of them since, but twenty years later that first pair still lie intact on the top shelf of my shoe rack; like jazz musicians they have improved with age because they have a kind of eternal, ugly grace.

The brothel creeper spirit will be with me until the day I die. They remind me of life before I became a mother when the maternal body is mapped in fluids – tears, blood, milk, just as that counter–tenor sang. I wore them to write my novels, to teach, to almost get married in Rome and then at the last minute, to run away. My beautiful brothel creepers remind me that getting older means you become the people you once mocked.

I sometimes wear socks.

A Purse of One's Own
Carol Shields

My mother's handbag, the one that I remember best, was big and black and aggressively pleated, with an enchanting amber clasp in the form of twin parrots. The bag's richly dark interior held the mingled fragrance of perfume and leather – calfskin, probably – and a cotton handkerchief dabbed with 'Evening in Paris' wadded in one corner.

Her bag smelled, too, of coins and creased bills, of the finely composted silt of face powder (Coty), and of tobacco crumbs (Chesterfields), and the roll of butter rum Life Savers that she always kept on hand to cancel out the smell of cigarettes on her breath. Her fountain pen would inevitably have leaked a stiff circular stain on the bag's taffeta lining. Her key ring – house, garage, car – bore the souvenir tag of the Wisconsin Dells, and in my memory she is forever rummaging in the depths of her bag for those keys, mumbling a self-scolding imprecation against carelessness, against disaster – and then, finally a rising gust of relief: 'I knew they were in here somewhere!'

We children were not allowed to go into our mother's handbag. If we needed a quarter or so for an errand, we were instructed to fetch the bag from the hall table and bring it to her. I never questioned this privileged zone of privacy. It just seemed to me that it was a mother's natural right and not merely a means of protection against the small larcenies of children. A women's handbag, I understood even then, was part of her being, an extension of her style and her soul, spiritual partner to her hat, her gloves, her everyday pumps. Later I came to suspect that the inside of a handbag is also the single inviolable space a woman possesses, other than the labyrinth of her own thoughts.

Why else would I have been so shaken by an unfortunate episode three years ago in Paris? I had entered a ticket gate in the Montparnasse metro station. I was filled with tourist zeal and a sense of well-being, yet a moment later my money and credit cards were gone. A stranger, someone without a face or form, had with great speed and cunning come up behind me, unzipped my handbag, and removed my wallet.

The shock lingered for days. I was grossly inconvenienced and embarrassed by the theft, not to say impoverished, but the emotional impact of the event outdistanced any sense of common robbery. At night in my Paris hotel room, I replayed the scene over and over in my head: I had inserted my ticket in the turnstile, pushed the security gate forward, and the next minute, aware only of a lightening of my shoulder bag and of a human shadow behind me, I was without my little cache of wealth, without my identity. For who was I without my portable clutch of documents and possessions? No one.

I must have been five or six when I was given my first 'bag', a stiff little box, lightly padded and covered with tan Leatherette. At that time I had no idea that Leatherette was a trademark for artificial leather, imagining instead that it was leather in its most rarefied and desirable form. A recently discovered family photograph confirms that this small bag was carried on a thin strap, not over my shoulder, but around my neck so that it lay flat on my chest. The closure, two golden knobs that turned satisfyingly one on the other, would have opened to nothing but rattling space, or perhaps a tiny ironed handkerchief and a Sunday school nickel. What else does a young child need to carry about? We might almost define childhood as that singular era in which there is no need to carry *things*.

But this possession-free period soon comes to an end. I was given, a few years later, a pencil case: a slim, zippered envelope of shiny green postwar plastic in which to carry my pencils and erasers, a few coins, and a compass-and-protractor set whose use would not be demonstrated for a number of years hence — but which I felt obliged to carry nevertheless. At the school I attended, only the girls carried these pencil cases, which can be thought of, I suppose, as handbags in their embryonic form: training purses. I remember that at twelve or thirteen we were highly conscious of their role as accessories, full of sharp pride and envy about the intricacies of their design. They mattered. A large, lonely girl named Charlotte was greatly pitied because her pencil case had been embroidered by her Danish grandmother and looked utterly unlike ours. Mary Ellen, on the other hand, queened over the rest of us with a neat pink case stamped with hula dancers. Fashion, that mystery, that consolation, was opening before us.

By the time we reached high school we were all, every one of us, equipped with a small *cordé* clutch bag in black or navy. We did not actually clutch these bags, but carried them instead atop our stacks of books, affecting great nonchalance when snapping them open in the girls' washroom and extracting a newly purchased Yardley lipstick in a fresh raspberry shade. *Cordé* bags were made flat, but the number of our *things* was growing. Now we carried, besides our make-up, a comb and mirror, chewing gum, perhaps even — if we were that kind of girl — a pack of cigarettes and a lighter. I had with me at all times a tightly folded copy of my latest sonnet; I was already known among my friends as a writer type, and these were the years of compulsive sonnet writing, one or two tossed off every week, sometimes more. They were my crossword puzzles, I see now, more a distraction from teenage stress than acts of creativity.

As we moved from freshman to senior year, our *cordé* bags became round and heavy like little bombs. The fabric gave way; they went shabby around the edges. We threw them away.

I was twenty when my mother took me to buy my first shoulder bag. This was the mid-1950s, when shoulder bags had been off the fashion list for years, but I was going to Europe to study, my junior year abroad, and my mother seemed convinced that a quality bag was essential for the security of my belongings. Perhaps she believed too in some unarticulated way that it might also protect *me*. A travel bag meant serious leather, an inconspicuous design, and a capacious interior. And, of course, there must be a zippered compartment, well hidden, for my passport. The Cold War was raging; there were people 'out there' who would kill for an American passport, which, according to current mythology, would bring thousands, even millions, on the black market.

We found the perfect bag in a downtown department store. The price was $11. My mother handed over her charge plate, and turned to me murmuring, as she always did when shopping, 'Now, don't tell Daddy how much it cost.'

But on the day we brought the lovely new shoulder bag home we neglected, for some reason, to remove the price tag before my father returned from work. There it sat on the dining-room table, still in its tissue paper. My mother and I watched as he inspected the stitching inside and out and checked the clasp. Then he regarded the price tag. 'Well,' he said at last, 'this is a very good bag. And a very good price too.'

I let go of my breath. My mother was not culpable, nor was I. The sense of relief I felt stayed with me. (Men, I saw, were not, after all, a race of fragile beings who had to be protected from consumer knowledge. They could bear the full force of truth, just as women did.)

*

A new handbag announces a new stage of life. You move into it, along with your personal documents, your cosmetics, your four-leaf clover, your knitting, your photograph of your sister's children. You might even sift through your belongings and decide to get rid of those two corroded French coins at the bottom of the old bag, or an expired library card from a city where you no longer live. (Why not toss out that baffling voucher for the free pound of coffee while you're at it?) The scribbled lists can go, too, with their mysterious gestures to the randomness or banality of forgotten errands: 'pedicure, red cabbage, candles, fleece, pills, oil.' Old movie stubs, gone soft as velvet, can be scooped up and jettisoned. A new bag signals lightness, order, resolution. We are able to reinvent ourselves with a simple purchase.

I've hated some of my bags. A white, zippered summer number abraded my wrist every time I reached into it. An immense square-cornered battle-ax of a bag refused to wear out. I've noticed that some very expensive bags tend to be excessively ugly, loaded down with tassels, jewels, gold appliqué, or clanking chains, the finest leather polished and quilted so that it acquires the precise look of bargain plastic.

Handbags are sometimes thought of as repositories of vanity, loaded with personal mementos or grooming aids. In fact, women's bags are more likely to be stocked with items that nurture and care for others: aspirin, Band-Aids, antihistamines, safety pins, needle and thread, a Swiss Army knife (for picnics? for an emergency tracheostomy?), a roll of cough drops, tampons, scissors, a small toy for a fractious child, clear nail polish to stop a run (anyone's run), a wet facecloth in a plastic bag, and probably, in years past, a bottle of smelling salts. (Just in case.)

I'm envious of those who seem able to manage with a chic little backpack or even a whippet of a bum bag. But I'm attached to the handbag as I know it, and I don't doubt that I will become more and more attached. I've observed how elderly women are never far from their bags, how they cradle them in their laps or attach them to their walkers or wheelchairs, as though all their lives were bundled within.

In the old days when a woman bought a new handbag, it came packed tightly with coarse gray paper. And in the midst of all the paper wadding there was always a little unframed rectangle of mirror. These were crude, roughly made mirrors, I remember, and I'm not sure people actually used them. They were like charms, good luck charms. Or like compasses. You could look in them and take your bearings. You could locate yourself in the world.

The Basque
A L Kennedy

The basque. It wasn't like me, not like me at all. That was the greater part of its appeal. I was – I think – twenty-one or -two, not so terribly far away from the rigours of school uniform and pretty much immersed in student dressing. I was used to wearing what was warm and cheap and relatively impervious to a range of malign and quixotic launderettes. British Rail, Her Majesty's Prison's and several European armies still supplied a good proportion of my wardrobe. So lingerie wasn't exactly my thing. Then came the basque.

Well, not exactly. Then came the man, would be more precise. And then the quickening slip into make-up, dresses, blouses, impractical shoes: the costumes for a largely one-track mind. Of course, other women could dress like this all the time, but I found I couldn't, didn't, had no wish to. I wore what I wore because of him, because of what I thought I wanted from him, because of what he seemed to want from me. Our arrangements had nothing to do with friendship or domesticity.

I was kitted out to match our best guess at mutual intentions: seduction as theatre with as little time as possible spent off-stage. Of course, today I wouldn't claim this constituted anything like a relationship, but then it was all I'd got and, naturally, it had its gymnastic compensations and, like any good obsession, was beguilingly intense. Still, I think I always knew I should have gone elsewhere and found something more relaxing and mundane, something genuinely shared between two partners, but equally my own. Because I did realise that most of the posturing and paraphernalia – even the passion – wasn't actually *mine*. Very little of what I wore or pretended to be had a firm connection with who I was or wanted to be. With perhaps predictable perversity, one of the few exceptions to this was the basque.

It was like an embrace. Not a *hug*, very definitely an *embrace*: a cool, sophisticated constriction, smooth on the skin and then warming to a firm, sleek secret under other, more ordinary cloth. Pleasantly sly when out of sight, it made posture and movements more formal and reserved while unbuttoning the mind and will entirely. Which is hardly surprising – nothing about it was designed to prolong its *staying* out of sight.

Even buying the thing was a heightened and vaguely surreal experience. I was – still am in many ways – a modest person. Huddled in a fitting room, preparing to try the basque on, I realised I hadn't been so seriously and semi-publicly un-dressed since the dreadful, clammy afternoons of schoolgirl swimming lessons. But there I was, almost entirely stripped in a talcum-scented cubicle, the meditative silence of a lingerie department thrumming all around. Initially, I was clumsy, worrying away at the strangely stiffened garment like a drunken interloper, unsure of which end to start with, wrestling with a recalcitrant progression of hooks and eyes.

And then the basque began to cover me, hold me tight. I stared at myself in the mirror, for the first time discovering that a basque is one of the few things in life that looks absolutely exactly the way it feels – quite wonderful.

I was startling in reflection, almost unbearably feminine. With the addition of only one garment I'd been entirely transformed into that very specific type of woman – the Bond girl, saucy postcard, late night type that I had always assumed had an extra chromosome on me. I looked, beyond anything else, *convincing*.

And, in matters of sex, I've always had to be convinced. My mind still needs to be cajoled, excited, tickled free before anything else can follow it. The basque, rather than the man, sadly provided my earliest demonstration of how quickly my intellect and Calvinist self-consciousness can be stunned into happy silence. It only takes the right sensation and the right idea: the right pressure on my thinking, my most influential erogenous zone.

My basque was correctly tender, was a beautifully eloquent thought in satin black. It introduced me to the difference between simply being desired and believing myself to be desirable. Its sensuality appealed to me, its lessons of repression and release. Here it controlled flesh, kept it pleasantly confined: elsewhere it left me tangibly exposed, complicitly free. The visual power it exploited came from every possible sleazy corner of objectified sex, but then it gave that power to me, handed over that guaranteed sensuality, with or without the intervention of an observer.

Although, needless to say, intervention did take place. At which point I learned that a great deal of the basque – if not sex itself – was about anticipation. We had our moments, I'm sure – almost everyone does – but consider how baffling even experienced, dextrous, small-handed men can find the fastenings of a basic brassière. For the purpose of removal, a basque represents a bra multiplied by twenty. Having made the perfect photograph, the entrance to make other entrances guaranteed, it seemed I should then provide bolt cutters, or just a Stanley knife. Careless disassembly broke the image and the moment. I won't make any pat assumptions about my heart.

And you won't be surprised to learn that for many reasons, very few of them sartorial, the man I had dressed for and I parted company. For months I kept wearing the pinching skirts, the shoes I couldn't walk in, the little dresses and the long coats. But I never even looked at the basque.

Then I began to rediscover my own taste. Slowly, I binned or gave away almost everything in my wardrobe that had been in any way connected with him. Only the basque stayed untouched at the back of a drawer. I started to dress for comfort – the very quietest manifestation of sensuality – and for many years my life was, physically, almost silent. Finally I threw the basque away.

I have wanted men since, been with men since, enjoyed their skin, their touch, but now I find I've lost the knack of dressing to celebrate my sexual presence, present with their own. It seems I can no longer risk the public show, enjoy that type of visual commitment. Perhaps this is a sign of timidity or approaching middle age. Perhaps it's simply a love of touch; of contact uninterrupted by costume. Perhaps it's only lack of practice and, one day, I will find my own way back to that particular strength, that particular delight in anticipation that I once felt, satin tight, in the touch of the basque.

The Pleasure of Pyjamas
Hiromi Goto

I am not a beautiful Asian. I am not beautiful. There is a difference between petite and short and one is considered more attractive than the other. Don't get me wrong, I'm not bitter about my lack of perceived physical beauty. My beauty lies beneath a tough surface, like a pomegranate, my Okasan is fond of telling me. Slither thinks all I need is a good orthodontist, a professional make-over and a haircut that isn't done with a pair of toenail scissors. Maybe she's right, but I refuse to succumb to the lure of pursuing superficial passions. Especially a passion that's created by people who don't look like me.

I am not beautiful, but I have the most expansive collection of pyjamas in the western hemisphere.

I found out a long time ago that clothing does not fit me. My big-boned arms, my daikon legs, my beta beta feet and splaying toes. My bratwurst fingers and non-existent neck. And my head. My poor colossal head, too huge to even dream of a ten gallon hat. It was excruciating torture when what clothes I'd finally found started threading into tatters. I held out as long as I could until even Dad noticed that the state of my unravelling, if unchecked, would lead to public nudity.

Get some clothes! he shouted. Then turned to my Okasan. What kind of mother was she! Couldn't she even raise her own kids properly? I sighed, turned my money socks inside out and picked out linted coins to roll into dollar bills.

I spent years of my life cursing the racks in the malls of despair. Jeans designed for long-legged hips. Slacks with no slack. Rugby pants were in for a while but not enough give across the butt. Knickerbockers had potential and portly men in the Baroque period didn't even look half bad. But they were out in six months and there was not another pair to be found. No matter what I wore, there was the pressing squeeze of material across my square body, the neck gaping lack of chest, pant hems trailing behind me like a bridal train. I buttoned, squeezed, choked, sweated years of snarling at lovely sales-clerks, crying in the changing rooms. Until I stumbled across a pyjama store closing down on its opening day, because no one was interested.

OPENING/CLOSING SALE! SALE! SALE!

I wasn't a pyjama person, and slept in only boxer shorts, but I was taken in by the sign. Could almost picture the mouth of the store opening and closing, gasping for clients it would never have. Like a giant fish trapped inside the mall aquarium but with no water, no oxygen.

I thumped inside and three clerks glided to me, eyes glowing and hair flowing like they were underwater. Glossy as mermaids.

'Welcome to the first and last day of "The Pleasure of Pyjamas"' they purred.

'Just looking,' I said curtly – force of habit after years of clothing torment.

The fresh-looking boy with one blue eye and one green eye, and the gingerskin woman with exquisite features glided away, discreetly, without leaving a ripple in their wake. The tall plain-haired woman lingered. Not invading the large space I needed around my person to feel comfortable, but just on the outskirts, gently present. She was plain as Wonderbread, plain as mashed potatoes. But there was this certain something – as soon as she opened her lips to talk, I was drowning in memories, sweet and evocative. The air that flowed from her mouth, the scent of her breath as pure as an infant's, like breastmilk, like dew on spring-fresh grass and sun-warmed peaches peeled by someone you love. I swirled in the sweetness of her breath, slow drowning and smiling.

'If I can help you in any way, please don't hesitate to ask. I'm Genevieve,' she smiled back.

'You've helped me already,' I said, then blushed, because it sounded so absolutely clichéd, and I hadn't realized until after I'd said it. And she would have no idea what I was referring to. But she was gracious.

'I'm glad,' she breathed, and went over to arrange a rack that had no need to be rearranged so that I was free to browse.

Blushed burning face. Geek, I thought to myself, dork, but my embarrassment didn't stop me from trying to think of things to say. Any excuse to stand in the perfume of her words, but not a chance. My swirling senses in no condition to conjure clever words, I turned to the shelf along the wall, pretending to look at pyjamas instead.

I ran my fingers along some material, and stopped. Cool, liquid silk beneath my skin. I really looked at the clothing I was touching and gasped at the colours.

Blue-green the depth of mountain lakes, swirling with black that would swallow stars. I could almost plunge into the colours and never surface. I pulled the pyjama top from the shelf and shook, it shimmering in my hands like water. Clasped the bottoms and held them against my body. Hands trembling, was led to a changing room, lapping at the sweet smell of Genevieve's breath.

There wasn't a mirror inside the room, and I had to step outside to see how I looked. But some magic clothed me. Unselfconscious, I stepped from the protection of the cubicle

23

and stood proudly under the glare of spotlights, in front of three hinged mirrors and three mermaids.

'It's you,' Genevieve breathed, and I swallowed at her words, their intoxicating scent. The pyjamas weaving some strange magic and I was lost. I was found.

Note
'The Pleasure of Pyjamas' is an extract from a novel in progress.

In Praise of the Body
Joan Smith

On the way back to London last summer after a holiday in the hills above Lake Trasimene, I stopped in Milan for an afternoon. It was a searingly hot August day and I stood for a while in the shade of the arcades which flank the cathedral square, peering up at the Gothic splendour of the *duomo*. Could I stand the heat long enough to take the lift to the roof, where office workers sunbathe among the gargoyles and crenellations? Without taking a conscious decision I found myself walking past the *duomo* to a tea shop, where I ordered a slice of stupendous white chocolate gateau. When there wasn't so much as a crumb left, I paid the bill and headed not for a gallery or a church but for a lingerie shop, where I happily spent the rest of the afternoon.

I love Italian underwear and when I finally emerged, I had in my hand a carrier bag which contained a perfectly exquisite confection, lovingly wrapped in tissue paper. Made from black lace, with underwired bra cups and high-cut legs, it's one of the most beautiful garments I've ever owned – underwear which, like Madonna's Gaultier corset, just begs to be worn to parties. It looks fabulous under a little black suit, with the jacket falling open, or worn with sheer black tights and high heels under a long-sleeved, ankle-length dress made from crushed chiffon. Wherever I'm going, I know I'll feel better the moment I slip it on – even if I'm the only person who knows I'm wearing it. It's not an everyday piece of underwear but I have lots of similar garments, neither so glamorous nor so ruinously expensive, for other occasions.

The person I have to thank for this transformation – for years I wore almost no underwear at all – is Donna Karan, the New York designer who is credited with inventing the body (or bodysuit, as Americans call it). In an industry dominated by men who are into hooker chic, or who appear to design clothes exclusively for women who look like boys, Karan is a magnificent exception – not just my favourite designer but the one who finally came up with underwear for grown-up women. I stopped wearing bras when I was eighteen or nineteen, and I remember how daring it seemed at the time to throw them away – a liberation in every sense of the word. No more straps sliding down arms at inconvenient moments, no more checking in mirrors to see whether they showed under a skimpy dress. But what I recall above all is the sensuous touch of fabric, a cotton T-shirt or silk blouse, against my bare breasts.

I'm not sure whether I had heard of bra-burning, which eventually became a lazy shorthand in newspapers and magazines for feminism, but going without a bra, for me, was undoubtedly a feminist statement. A rejection of conventional femininity, which was summed up by Marilyn Monroe in a pointy bra a generation before, it certainly wasn't a refusal of *sexuality*. Far from it. Going bare-breasted seemed much sexier – and attention-grabbing – than squeezing myself into some ill-fitting garment from Dorothy Perkins or Marks & Spencer, the shops from which I and my friends acquired our underwear in those days. No Knickerbox, certainly no Agent Provocateur, and most of the bras on offer came in white, flesh tones or a nondescript shade called ecru.

I *hated* them. I didn't care for knickers much either, but I especially loathed the effect of bra and pants together – the way they divided a woman's body up, like tight-fitting bandages, as if she had been cut in half and badly reassembled. Bras, for me, were an unacceptable form of bondage and I dispensed with them; something I could get away with easily because I have smallish breasts. When I reluctantly bought one again, many years later, it was only because I was going to dance classes and felt uncomfortable without any support at all.

What had happened, I now think, was that my body shape and my perception of myself had been changing for some time. I was wearing more tailored clothes and when I finally got round to being measured in Selfridge's lingerie department, I discovered I was a 34C rather than my old size of 32B, something the contraceptive pill may have been responsible for. I realised that underwear had changed during my long abstention from it; that there were far more underwired bras than I remembered, and that there was altogether more lace, more decoration, and a lot more black. But I still didn't like bras much.

Then I discovered, the body. All-in-one, with narrow straps and a discreet fastening between the legs, it took me back to a semi-punk period in my life when I used to go to parties wearing what used to be called a leotard, along with high heels and a man's shirt borrowed from my then boyfriend – the kind of thing I imagined Debbie Harry wore to New York discos when she wasn't touring with Blondie. (How feminists ever got a blanket reputation for hating sex or decorative clothes is something I've never managed to figure out. Did anyone ever look at what we were wearing?)

The first body I bought, second time round when they had acquired a name, was plain, black, and long-sleeved. The next was tight-fitting, with lots of seams around the breasts – the nearest thing to underwiring I'd ever owned. I liked it so much that I decided to visit a lingerie shop for the first time in my life, leaving with a little black number I couldn't wait to wear. Instead of cutting my body in two ungainly halves, it emphasised curves and made me feel sexy in much the way I did, ironically enough, when I abandoned nasty white nylon bras years before.

Now my wardrobe is full of bodies, from a crushed black velvet version by Donna Karan to the black lace ones by La Perla which I tend to buy in Italy, where they're slightly cheaper. I wear them with jeans and under big sweaters as well as party dresses and I even cook in them, sometimes greeting dinner party guests before I realise I've forgotten to finish dressing. Who cares? The Metropolitan Museum in New York held an exhibition four or five years ago called 'Underwear as Outerwear', so I'm in good company. The only thing that puzzles me, years after I abandoned bras, is why it took so long for someone to invent a piece of underwear that's wearable, sexy, *and* I can answer the front door in.

High Hopes
Caryn Franklin

I find it hard to remember why I was *ever* so attracted to such a monstrous pair of shoes, but I'll try.

I think it's important to state here and now that I haven't worn my silver wedge peep-toe platform sandals, procured from Petticoat Lane for the price of several weeks' Saturday pay, for twenty-five years – well not out of the house. But I do keep them close by.

In fact I can see them as I write – great blocks of footwear with enough cork filling to tile a medium sized bathroom floor, with more to spare for matching drinks coasters. They were, and still are, the shoe world's equivalent of mirrored office blocks. On my feet back in 1974, they provided a high-rise experience, lifting me a clear six inches from the pavement and allowing for lofty exchange with ordinary urban travellers.

In pedestrian terms, they weren't practical and those Hounslow streets turned into a concrete obstacle course every time I left my front door. For cycling purposes, it would be fair to say that my strappy wedges were ill-suited. But, I was determined to overcome such tiresome limitations in order to achieve elevated status amongst my girl friends.

Those plucky fashion items were responsible for the only row my parents and I ever had about clothes. Liberal types that they were, I enjoyed relative freedom of dress. Lashings of plummy lip and lid gloss, red halterneck top and wide Oxford bags did not raise an eyebrow as I left for school in the morning (even if I was sent home by lunchtime). But the shoes managed to cause a rift, and on safety grounds alone, they were banned. Not to be hemmed in by such unimaginative restraint, I loaded my comedy footwear into a Macfisheries bag and cycled out of view where I duly changed from lowly plimsolls to state-of-the-art wedges.

I would not relinquish this chance to appear immaculately accessorised and perfectly presented in a post-pubescent kind of way. My platforms were my confidence, my world, my only choice of footwear. Undeterred by the fact that I had to walk with my gaze directed floorward so as to spot any minute change in level, or even by members of the public hanging out of their cars to laugh, I strode majestically the length and breadth of Treaty Road during my fifteenth summer, eagerly awaiting favourable comment from a like-minded male fashion pundit. Regrettably this did not happen and I prefer to think that in all my fake Biba glory, I was a paragon of stylish cool and therefore unapproachable – scary even. The fact that I was nearly six foot two in my designer stilts may have prevented a love interest from approaching, and come to think of it, my boyish contemporaries with their squeaky voices and fluffy faces, had visibly shrunk with this latest fashion. Their stacked heels, it seems, provided insufficient boost to counter feminine trends.

The joy of towering above them all, surveying my community with unaccustomed superiority, was my first taste of power. It was compromised just slightly by the fact that, like a driver in a posh car, I could not proceed rough shod through urban terrain without due caution. With practice, however, I could perform a passable canter and even managed to descend stairs without snatching desperately at the banister. And there were unforeseen benefits. After a freak summer shower I enjoyed wading through the centre of a large obstructive puddle and spent the rest of the day proving to myself and other soaked shoppers, that up against the odd monsoon, I was fashionably in control.

Yep, those shoes were like family to me, and as I looked in the mirror one evening before setting off to a teen gathering, I silently pledged never to sabotage my style on some petty whim of the fashion industry. I had found my look, complete with satin bomber jacket, three button high waister trousers and cardboard hair. How could anyone, I thought as I gyrated earnestly that night, fail to be impressed by the marvellously groomed goddess in front of them?

Then one day it happened. And as I look at my silver skyscrapers, quietly enduring the decades with at least more dignity than a Bay City Roller single, I can only relive the moment with a pang of resignation.

To say that my body, or more precisely my feet, let me down would only be half the story, but it would be the portion that rankled the most. Winter inevitably set in, and the harsh biting wind warranted performance clothing. Out went the flimsy bomber jacket with repeat print rainbows and clouds, and in came a longish forties style smock coat with enormous lapels and an overly large check print. Lined it was not, but trendy – well that was the only criterion in my day. For feet, I chose something high and booted from Shepherd's Bush Market and , pedalled with conviction.

The silver slippers would have to winter at the back of the wardrobe until a comeback was deemed seasonally appropriate. But imagine my pique the following April when I discovered that a sudden growth movement had separated me from my precious pedestals. Now a larger size. I could no longer fit into my beautiful shoes without toe and heel surplus. The fact that my peers seemed to have climbed down, quite literally, and could now be seen prancing about in daintier and altogether less troublesome designs was unnerving. I had grown used to conversing with them about tights, netball, lager and black, parents, French kissing, hockey and David Bowie. Now suddenly I was looking at the tops of their heads and bending to catch a few words. I couldn't keep up during breaks when others raced off to the ROSLA (Rising Of School Leaving Age) block, to hang around with the sixteen year olds who had been forced by law to spend another year at school.

In fact, as I stood in front of a shoe store window contemplating my summer shoe purchase a whole year later, I genuinely believed that my best posing days were over. The chance to stand head and shoulders above my male contemporaries was lost, never to be repeated again, and my lone desire to rise to nostalgic heights was certainly not aided by the new season's low-slung slip-ons. Why did Linda, Marion and Yvonne want to occupy the same base airspace as our surly friends with testosterone meltdown, I queried, as I sank my foot into something unspeakably restrained. It was a mystery then, and, as fashion statements go, it would be on a par with my reluctance, a decade later, to bin my aged Johnson's biker boots complete with dog chains, spikes and an unnecessary number of blakeys.

Clothing is like armour to me. Swathed in layers of textile defence, I am a she-warrior. Today in the boardroom, the chance to appear matt black, shiny and impenetrable is mine with the help of a well-cut suit and scraped back hair and, as I get dressed for such events, I am reminded of my earlier allegiance to the power shoe. Of course times have changed. In the footwear department neither metallic sandal tanks nor combat boots with the ability to gore hostile parties fits the bill. But, before I step into the arena armed with womanly experience, a whiff of Eau D'Issey and a briefcase full of facts, I steal a loving look at these platforms and remember the sheer joy of striding out with my head in the clouds.

The Colour of Death
Manju Kak

I always had a sense of the past, sniffing at it in the old rusted locks of my mother's dowry trunks, lodged in the iron cage inside a small dark room that smelt cold, dingy and of mothballs. A cage built for a panther's cub Nana had found on one of his *shikar* trips. I often wondered why, out of all my brothers and sisters, why I alone, had this haunting sense of the past?

Could I have been a princess? In my last life? I ask my mother who hears me like a faint echo through the mist of her dopey daze. Of course, she murmurs, a real princess. My seven-year-old chest is expanding as I hold my breath in tight and I put a corkscrew on it. Inside me, I can feel it growing, the princess. The cage door is ajar. The rusted locks, open. Her eyes are closed as my faded mother gently snores on the shady veranda. I tiptoe into the cage. I am a princess in a cage. I prise the trunk open. Inside it are satin and chamois silks with delicate flowery embroidery, saris that Parsee merchants brought in wooden ships built at the Sassoon Docks. Ships that sailed from Canton to Bombay, where my mother's aunt purchased them, one by one, for her. Crocodile leather trunk creaks open further, the eye still closed. More saris come tumbling out; Benaras tissues, a gossamer weave of tiny paisleys and delicate *bootis*, cottons and *chanderis*, salmon skies after rains have fled, embroidered with green parrots twittering in mango groves, navy organza festooned with green and gold *zari* stars in a midnight moonless sky, the rainbow woven into silks, peacocks spreading feathers in monsoon mating dances. Dower enough for a princess.

Scarlet lipstick, a chalk mark across my blackboard face, I drape them across me, one by one. I am a princess in silk, in satin; hyacinth, cyclamen, honeysuckle, wistaria – shades of the flowers that grow in the manicured beds of my boarding school. I look into my mother's Burma-teak, Belgian-glass dressing table, another piece of magnificent dower Nana endowed her with. Her father, my Nana, stares down from the photo of him reflected in the window of my mind: fierce blue eyes turned icy under the heat of a Gangetic plain; her, my mother, standing behind his chair; me, I, infant, last born, in his strong arms. Arms that sprang out from a legendary fifty-two inch chest. I don't believe it, I whisper to my brother who, an inch tape in his hand, is measuring the girth of a set of long johns that he has foraged from Nana's cabin trunk, a remnant of a voyage he took out in a P&O, when he retired as District Collector of Basti. First I will go to London he announced grandly, to Savile Row, to equip myself and then I shall travel the Continent. Venice and Rome, Vienna and Salzburg.

The cabin trunks when opened after his death were overflowing with shirts, breeches, cuff links, ties, cravats, tie presser, cuffs, hankies that he never ever wore. Just old clothes! my mother says to my father when Nana's baggage arrives. But all new, he exclaims. Returned from his maiden voyage a man of saffron? Head to foot a *sadhu*, never needing those fine cottons and woollens, shirts, breeches and long johns he had purchased to equip himself?

Mysteries mysteries, unsolved mysteries, and now I, princess, with a haunting sense of the past, pushing aside my tape-measuring brother, am pirouetting in front of the mirror, with a cravat from my Nana's cabin trunk, come all the way from far off London, or a cyclamen sari from Canton. They can make me become anything. Gold topped cane in hand and I'm a Lord walking in Hyde Park, or...? Prince, princess? which shall *I* be?

Just a change of dress, it was so easy then.

Shall I ride in a chariot with a flaming sword or shall I wear cyclamen, Ma? And she, sleeping on a *charpoy*, she tired, always tired and faded, always sleeping on a *charpoy* in the shady veranda, murmurs with her one eye open, safer daughter to be a prince. Her eyes remain closed, they don't open, why won't they open? Mama, mama, open your eyes, my brother and I whisper.

They are crying, they are draping her body with a white sheet, they are crying even more and calling me poor child, poor child. I am sitting near my mother's white body and asking why she is sleeping? Why does she carry on sleeping? Why is my mother clothed in a white sheet? And then he comes in white *dhoti*, his *janau* upon his chest, and he begins to chant and suddenly all of the women are wearing white and they are like swans, the swans in my picture book and these swans are bathing my mother, annointing her, and draping her in red silk, and saying the gods have blessed her, she died a *suhagin*, and they are putting red vermilion in the parting of her hair to show how fortunate she was not to have died a widow and saying she will surely go to heaven. Why was my mother in faded white on the *charpoy* alive and my mother in red silk dead?

I quickly shut the cabin trunk spilling with Nana's clothes from the west. I close Mama's dowry bower with its eastern fare. I shut the two trunks tightly and turn the rusted key upon the rusted locks and close up my life.

I will not be a princess mother, I will not be a prince.

But I will wear a salwar kameez and go to college, and wear spectacles on my nose and read books to learn about life. I will not wear your cyclamen sari with the rambling wistaria any more. I will wear the mask of forgetfulness and then, maybe, then, I will begin to *learn* why you needed to wear red to die. Yes, maybe then, I will begin to *understand* why, the colour of your life was faded... but faded not, the colour of your death?

Glossary

shikar – hunt

bootis – motifs

chanderis – fine silk fabric

zari – gold and silver thread weave

sadhu – saint

charpoy – string cot

dhoti – traditional male dress

janau – caste thread

suhagin – to die in a married state, considered auspicious

The Lady in the Boat
with the Red Petticoat

Jean Buffong

It's strange how for no obvious reason some things surface in your brain.

As I rummaged around trying to decide what to wear for the evening's event a riddle emerged from somewhere in my mind: 'the lady in the boat with the red petticoat'. Just that, nothing more. Why this should come into my head at that time, I didn't give it a thought. It was just there.

I wanted to look 'good' for the evening. But to me looking good means firstly feeling good, not dolled up like a dog's dinner and feeling uncomfortable. After doing an in-house fashion show, the only thing I felt really good in at that moment was a light shimmering pink coloured satin nightshirt; temptation. It was difficult to decide *what* to wear. I expected most people there, especially the 'speaky spoky' ones, to be dressed up to the nines. I emptied my wardrobe. Everything was strewn in heaps on the floor and on the bed. The outfit I had bought for the evening was laid out at one end of the bed...a nearly-silk light cream designer suit, co-ordinated shirt, matching handbag and shoes. But at the last minute that did not feel right. I felt bumpy and lumpy and simply not right.

My daughter came in just as I slid into a slinky black slimline dress, well the dress is slimline anyway – as for me a roll here and there fitted more adequately. 'Mummy,' she said, 'you look great, but isn't it a bit much. Who're you expecting to meet. I mean it...'

'I know what you mean.' I glanced across at her in time to see the cheeky grin hiding behind her eyes. 'You can never tell, one must always be prepared.'

'What about this one?' she said, holding up a forest-green exquisitely embroidered Nigerian gown. This was acquired through the generosity of a Nigerian friend. It was one of the most beautiful handmade outfits I had owned up till now. Every time I look at it it reminds me of the formation of birds in flight as they glide freely in the sky. Somehow this did not seem appropriate for that evening.

It was almost seven o'clock. I had to be at the Common-wealth Institute by eight o'clock. There was no time to go shopping. In any case this was the season of stagnant cash flow. I was getting a bit desperate.

After trying to convince me that the outfit I had on looked all right (without any luck), my daughter left me in the midst of my jumble. I looked around and sighed, and again became conscious of that riddle going through my mind, 'the lady in the boat with the red petticoat'. Just that, nothing else. I looked at the clock. Time to put something on.

In the end I chose a simple brown dress, made out of a cleverly patterned tie and dye cotton material. I slipped it over my head. The handbag and shoes I originally intended to use complemented it. I felt great. The dress brought back memories, pleasant memories. It was what one would call 'made to measure' only there was no real measuring involved.

It was our last shopping day in Serrunkunda market in the Gambia, West Africa. The sun was at boiling point intensified by the haggling, bartering and generally being part of the whole scene. During that week I had mastered the art of haggling, but the stall holders had years' headstart. That day I found myself boxed inside a stall; mountains of material of all colours and designs around me with the stall owner at the doorway determined not to let me out unless I bought something. It was a tricky situation. How could I get out with my dignity intact while not offending my 'sister'.

Then I had a brainwave. I'd challenge her. I told her that if she could make me two dresses in the space of half an hour, that was all the time we had left before returning to the hotel to pack, if she could make me two dresses within that time we could do business. It was a bluff. Not in my wildest dreams did I expect her to take up the challenge. She not only agreed to have them completed but would not expect to be paid unless they were done within the time and to my satisfaction. I was a bit dubious. Nevertheless I chose the material and told her what I wanted. Nothing fancy. The pattern of the material would be enough style ... No tape measure, no pins here and there, no fittings.

'Don't worry my sister,' she laughed, 'my son in the other stall, he has the sewing machine. It will be all right.' With that she went off leaving me holding the stall. Customers came and went. It was great fun being on the other side of the counter for a while. Less than half an hour later my wardrobe was increased by two beautiful handmade dresses. Nothing measured and shaped; only the patterns of the material conspicuously placed, a stitched snip for the neck, and side stitched to allow my arms airing space. It was just amazing.

Now, reflecting on how that dress was acquired made me feel even better. The cool cotton felt like gold against my bronze skin.

My escort had arrived. At last I was ready, but something was still missing. I did not know what it was. Everything was in order or seemed to be. Although I was completely dressed in an outfit I felt comfortable in, I still felt incomplete. I again checked everything and everywhere. I rummaged through my handbag. Nothing visible was missing. My earrings, rings, wrist watch, everything was in place, yet ... My escort was becoming impatient.

'The lady in the boat with the red petticoat,' there it is again, that riddle, only this time it went a bit further. 'The lady in the boat with the red petticoat. What is it?' Then it clicked.

'Just a minute,' I shouted, 'I have to get something.' I went into the kitchen, took from the shelf my large tin of whole spices. From there I extracted one solid, clean, perfectly patterned whole nutmeg and slipped it into my handbag. Great, I said to myself, great. Now my outfit is complete. Now I am ready for the evening.

As time has gone by, the nutmeg has become an important part of my clothing – an accessory, just like earrings, bangles and so on. It is not for its lovely fragrance because I prefer it unbroken; it's just that without a nutmeg in my bag I feel underdressed or even undressed. I am not sure why it started but that's how it is. It is not a good luck charm or anything like that, it is just part of my dressing. Having it in my handbag gives me a sense of being. It evokes childhood memories. In Grenada where I was born and at the time I was born the nutmeg was king, or should I say queen – whichever, it was the ruler... the economic ruler. I grew up claiming the nutmeg as part of my existence.

Among the many riddles and proverbs we learnt at school was one which gave a living image to the nutmeg. Someone would shout out, 'The lady in the boat with the red petticoat. What is it?' Someone else would shout out the answer, 'The nutmeg.' The lady is the actual nutmeg. The boat is the creamy pod; and the petticoat is the red lacy mace that surrounds the hard shell wherein lies the nutmeg. There is mystery surrounding the nutmeg layers, useful layers, to be unfolded before getting to the nut itself. It could be likened to a beautiful, mysterious, seductive lady.

Having a nutmeg as part of my accessories is very symbolic. Growing up in and then moving away from the island, it somehow represents the cord that binds me to home and so to me is a kind of completeness.

The last piece of garment in place, I stepped out like a queen. I think that is what the riddle was trying to say to me all along.

My Mother's Brooch
Janice Galloway

My family weren't hoarders. We didn't *hive* or *husband*, and
treasure was a noun for pirate use, not a verb. *Cherish* was a doll's
name and *souvenir* meant only stick of rock – for someone else.
I admit there were Christmas tree ornaments wrapped in
newspaper (not cotton wool) at the back of the hall cupboard,
but nothing else in our house was quite so conserved, so laid
down like wine. We didn't have wine. No cellars, basements,
loftspaces or, though we knew such things existed, attics. They
belonged to folk with cut-crystal voices and matching beads,
who stuffed them with mind-boggling things like rocking
horses, hand-embroidered christening robes, helmets dented
from the bullets and bayonets of interchangeable, un-named
wars. Attics were romantic, full of mustiness, mad aunts, and veils
of stoury grey muslin; the sanctuaries of children or people
with amnesia hiding from some truth too awful to know. In
books, films, wild imaginings, attics existed all right, but they
were not ours. Not mine. My things came from Corner
Duncan's or were knitted from Co-op wool after which they
wore out, lost their shape and/or got passed on to that woman
from Paisley who lived down the street, whose man battered
her and whose weans didn't even have socks. Hoarding – salting
away – spoke of something else entirely: a home with space,
things that lasted; a family where to care and say so was not
embarrassing or dangerous, it was *normal*. When I thought about
attics – and I did – I smelled powdered ginger, felt my cheek

against the squashy warmth of a cashmere-covered breast. When I grew up and won the Pools, I fancied, it would all come right. I'd have a white Harley Davidson, a white dress; this home, this family.

Meantime there were wardrobes and my mother's was full. She had nothing in cashmere, but she liked clothes and they liked her back. A scarlet coat, hat and shoes marked her out in shops, while weddings brought her out in shocking pink and royal; limes, nasturtiums and skies. She had a whole collection of Fair Isle suits, knitted entirely in four-ply by my sit-at-home sister, in matches of forests, sea-blues, autumn rubies and russets. She had earth-tone sepias and bruisy purples. She had indoor hats and outdoor hats, neat car-coats and winter snoods, scarves, patterned rain-mates, gloves and strings of chunky beads. The only colour she couldn't abide was yellow. She had nothing yellow, not a thing. *It makes me look like I died*, she'd say: *like I've gone cold*. Outside work, where she wore it every day as a dinner lady, white, too, was rare. It got dirty, needed *upkeep. White's all right if you've servants.* As for the rest of the colour spectrum, anything went and often did. Beautifully. She had, it was known locally, style.

It started in the North of England. My mother had been raised if not born there because her father and brothers were miners and that's where the coal was. In Darton. The youngest of seven, she watched all five brothers get cake at weekends while she and her sister had none, then she watched them all go down the pit. Lizzie went into service. My mother tried the mill but it cut her fingers, so she went into service too, where she learned to cry every night but dressed nice on days off to cheer herself up. Her employer took it as cheek. *Should've seen her stuff*, my mother sniffed: *I wouldny have put it out for jumble.* Lizzie gave her things, she said and not till she was dying and delirious, did she admit that some of them must have been stolen. Not then though. Then, the two girls got by, looked smart, vowed not to be their mother. They came back to Scotland looking for work that didn't make your fingers bleed or force you to board with bastards, and found something that made you smell of money. The buses. A clippie for years, my mother married her driver, settled in Saltcoats, and never got over the shock. *Saltcoats* she'd say, a bucket-and-spade economy. After a while, she looked back to Darton and wondered what she'd missed. My Uncle Jock was still there. He'd married a Yorkshire girl. He was mayor, for godsake. Jock and Louie sent Christmas cards, the odd letter, and, every so often, came to Saltcoats to tell my mother how much better everything was in England. Later still, when my Aunty Lizzie was only somebody my mother fought with and my dad was dead, she took me, the baby she'd thought was the menopause, on holiday to theirs. *Bloody Saltcoats*, she'd say, *it's only two weeks but it's away*.

I must've been seven the first time, my mother forty-eight. Jock would have been in his sixties. I remember him fat and taciturn with a Clark Gable moustache squint on his orange-peel upper lip. Louie was coarse and funny and blind with dyed yellow hair. She gave me pink sherbet you didn't get at home that made your eyes water and called it *snap*. *Doestha like snap?* she'd say and laugh for ten minutes, unfathomable. She called rolls *baps*, ate bread and dripping, rolled her phlegmy eyeballs and laughed all the time. *Say something Scotch*, she'd say, hooting: *else thee s'llavta fetch pig's blood from Allan's*. Haha. Allan's was round the corner and really did sell pig's blood. In cups. Out the back door, I shelled broad beans, avoiding the animal rub of the furry linings, shocked by how much of these alien pulses was redundant, so cavalierly chucked away. We ate at Jock's. My mother didn't like cafés: bowls of communal sugar with crusty spoons and dried-out mustard pots were *common as muck*. So we ate Louie's freshly killed Yorkshire standards, and bought them something at the end of the stay to prove we weren't mean. And where we bought — where everyone bought — was Barnsley.

Barnsley was not Darton. Darton had only a railway bridge and a moor, from what I remember. Barnsley, on the other hand, had a hotel. It had things to do at night, a bookshop, its glamorous, cosmopolitan market. We'd go early and spend eight till afernoon, trawling the market for sport, all the while my mother doing what she did all holiday only worse. She spoke Yorkshire. All the time. She spoke it to barrow boys and stall holders, tea-tent ladies and total strangers, wondering aloud why I was so quiet. We'd finger tea-towels, fire-tongs, porcelain figurines in shepherdess frocks, sheets and linger, covetous, over jewellery. Their jewellery was something special. Laid out on big flat tables glittering against green baize, it chilled to the touch, made your fingers smell of watery pebbles. Earrings were all right and beads – never necklaces – had their charm, but what caught the heart, could catch it for hours while my mother left me to it, were brooches; big picture brooches like stories inside gold frames. One stall had nothing but; brooches made of opalescent, pastel stones wrought with gold stuff, as animals, insects, bunches of unspecific flowers. Buds and eyes were picked out in diamanté chips, pins in safety-pin silver. Warmth spread through the alloy when you touched them: the biggest filling half a hand without weight. Occasionally, the stall holder held one up to the light, placed it against my school navy, confirming what I already knew. These brooches were the most beautiful things in the world. I stared, walked away, came back. Came back.

The oval frame spilling with milky-gold daisies, stems caught with a treble band of gold, every petal sun-like, every leaf a different degree of Georgian green, was still there. Heavy glue on the pin. It was built to last, regal, 2/9d. In its box and resting on cotton wool, it looked to me like authentic love. I hid the buying and took it all the way home before I gave it. Her face went the same soft way it did when she had powder on, then she caught herself, stopped it. *What did you do that for?*

she said, safely stony. *You shouldn't have wasted your money.* And
I noticed for the first time. It was yellow.

After she died, my sister and me turned up in tandem, not sure
what to do with each other, with three days to clear the house.
Council rules. Since it was important to show only the
traditional family emotion of nothing at all, the time-frenzy
was welcome. A van from a place that specialised in funeral
clearances took all the furniture, including the kitchen fittings
and the curtains, for £300. £300. Left only with her kitchen
bits, clothes, lipsticks and teeth, we were less sure. My sister
picked gingerly over the suits she had knitted, the hands that
once beat me till I bled still supple as a girl's. Horribly, her eyes
filled, so she thoughtfully pretended she was hungry and left
for lunch. I took two Fair Isles and left two for Nora when it
was my turn to do *lunch* later. That was all I could think of to
do. I could hear my own feet on the floorboards, the absent
noise of my mother cleaning. Improvising, pretending it
mattered, I did it myself. I loosened ancient fire lighters and
Brasso tins from cubby-holes, junked dusters made of vests and
limp packets of pan bread. Tidying up, I called it. It was always
what we called it. Flinging things away.

I found unsuspected bodice-rippers and detective
magazines under the bed and binned them. I dumped her
underwear in one without looking, tried not to notice its
powdered-ginger scent. The haze of Ajax and toilet blocks
under the kitchen sink came next; a solitary mouse-trap,
snapped shut on nothing. The bathroom cabinet, full of
ancient packets of Anadin, went out whole. The huge mound
of old *Ardrossan and Saltcoats Heralds*, some already twisted into
kindling, I boxed and tied with string. I found the Christmas
ornaments too right where they'd always been, past the hoover
and ironing board in the hall cupboard. Pulling them out, I
found something else, something right at the back. A big

margarine tub, catering size, opaque white plastic: most likely something from dinner-lady days. It hissed when I shifted it, a shifting-sand whisper. With bomb-disposal delicacy, I forked it into the light and prised up the lid. It was full of sugar. Little sachets, individual size, saved from godknew how many café saucers: dozens when I tipped them out, dozens of clean paper cushions, each printed with an Alpine flower. I poured them, ran my hands through the drift of crackly Eidelweiss, stared for a long time. She must have been stealing them, salting them away, for years. And nobody knew. This Swiss whiteness, this abundance. Nobody knew. Since the box was handy, I spilled the Christmas tree things out too, and there, wrapped in pale green toilet paper, eighteen years old, was the brooch. It looked like something that came free with a Barbie doll outfit, but it had lasted. The pin was firmly in place and the colour. was as strong as ever. Yellow. Indisputably yellow. Anyway.

Anyway, Nora was due back. And I'd made a mess. With my few minutes of remaining solitude, there was nothing left for it but to tidy that away too. The glass Santas and tear-drop baubles, the threadbare tinsel and dud lights went straight to the bin with the ashes from my mother's last fire. The brooch went too of course: job lot. That I should do the same with the sugar never entered my head. Sugar was not ornaments; it was useful. It was for tipping carefully back into the tub and giving to the woman at the end of the road. She was pleased and I told my sister nothing. It's what we do in our family. We say nothing we don't have to. But we pass things on. One way or another, we pass things on.

Whole Cloth
Susan Stinson

'When we look closely, or when we become weavers, we learn of the tiny multiple threads unseen in the overall pattern, the knots on the underside of the carpet.'

Adrienne Rich[1]

Once there was a small girl. She was small in height and years, that is, but her chin was full and her legs were thick and she was shaped like a drum. I see her sitting tight, with her thin tight dresses pulling across her chest, and her tight patterned trousers creasing her thighs.

The land around her was flat. The small girl played kickball on the grass with the others. She played softball, spud and time-to-find-the-midnight-ghost. She did not make out behind the little shed. She did take her clothes off there, privately, shutting the plank door with the good brass knob that her father had installed, sitting on the plywood floor in the bit of bare space between the bicycles and the lawnmower, leaning on a bag of peat moss. It smelled like grass and turpentine. She itched.

This was only on afternoons when everyone was out. She knew it was nasty.

Sometimes she sat in there and read Louisa May Alcott. Sometimes she just breathed. Sometimes she pulled off her stretchy blue shorts and her underpants. She left them dangling around her sneakers so it would be faster to pull her clothes back on if she heard someone coming.

She stood up and swung her hips a little, and moved her back. A little breeze crossed her, dry air passing between her fat thighs, soft against the places that got sore from sweating and rubbing in tight pants.

A neighbor's mower started up. She pulled her striped top off over her head, then felt too bare. She pulled her shoes and socks off with her feet, shaking the shorts from her ankles, then opened the door and stepped out on to the grass.

Naked. Now what? Her heart was hitting the inside of her chest. The grass felt familiar. She could see the oil stains on the concrete of the empty carport. What if the station wagon pulled in just then? What would her mother do? Forget the neighbors' windows. Run. She ran in a hot circle around the toolshed, past the garbage cans, then back in the door to strong smells and less light. She shut the door, breathed hard, leaned against the gasoline cans. Their rims pressed into her back. If she messed them up, her father would know that she had been in there. Better get dressed.

My blouse gapes. My zipper may not close. I make my fingers sore forcing it up. My sides and belly have a deep ridge in them after a day of that. My pants wear out on the inseam, thinning and splitting where my legs rub. I have to try to walk delicately, as if I met only at the crotch; as if the whole of my legs weren't intimate with each other, rubbing together just as my arms rest on my breasts and my breasts rest on my belly. The clothes can't get into every fold and separate every layer of flesh from itself. The dark blues can't camouflage me, the vertical stripes can't hide me, and no foundation garment can keep me in.

Look at this. This is a painting from around 1618. A fat woman did. it. It tells a story, but I won't tell it here. I'm not writing the story of the strong Jewish woman who chopped off the general's head, although that story needs to be taken and told. I'm not writing the story of her maidservant, whose name is never mentioned, who helps God make her mistress beautiful, who carries the food into the enemy camp, who watches by the door as Judith kills, who carries the head back in a basket, who is freed in a line of the last chapter. This is not her story, although her name needs to be found, her life remembered, and her deeds told. I'm not writing the story of the young Italian painter raped in her studio by her teacher and tortured in thumbscrews at the trial of her rapist. This is not her story; it's an image of one of her images.[2]

Arms. Hands. Light. A wide thigh. Small breasts. Two women look past the candle. A man's head is being handled. Judith is dressed up. One hand is held high, flat, shielding the candle, shadowing her face. With the other hand she holds a curved sword. Look at her belly, at the light up her arms, the geometry of it.

The maidservant tucks cloth around the severed head. Her own neck is thick and taut. Both women have double chins. The woman with no name, the maid, is crouching. Her scarf is light and has deep living folds, like a brain, like my back.

There's a lot of cloth in this picture. The figures are big.

The smell of sizing. The altered pattern in its envelope on the sewing chair. It's a half size. We have three yards of cloth. We stretch it across the dining-room table. I pull on the diagonal, move to change the angle, then pull again against my mother. We are straightening the grain.

Balance this with the two women in the painting. The arms. The tension. The light. Frame it in the sliding glass door, with long curtains.

We take the fact that we are fat and wrap it in cloth like an enemy's head, except we can't chop it off.

Those women in the story of the painting ate. The Bible tells me so. Even in the time of famine, they ate corn, figs, bread and cheese, with wine and oil. They look no thinner than my mother and I. They look no fatter than my mother and I. I don't know what the models ate. It does not matter to me.

It is beautiful, this picture of us stretching the cloth. There is passion in a long, taut fold of it between us. Our bellies touch the edges of the table as we lean over it.

My mother is helping me make a nice blouse. She has widened the pattern and will take the darts. She marks where they go with colored tracing paper and a spiked metal wheel. I love her. She calls me in to fasten her long-line bra. It takes all my strength to do this.

Two women dance. One wears a long scarf, silver and blue. Her black pants are loose and puff out across the form of her lower belly so that the waves in her body there, all of that loose rhythm, pass out through her fat and become subdued and muted in the fabric. Her big hips send out currents that cross the paths of motion from her shoulders and her back. She wears a red shirt. It shines. The red goes darker deeper back in the folds of her fat, then pulls bright and flat across her thicker places as the music pulls those hips up and they swing like power through the air, sending flutters down the pant legs. Her breasts fall like grace past the ends of her scarf.

The second woman wears no shoes. A new song starts. She is jumping, streaming color. Her feet lift. The music sparks. Her calves are bare and pale under dark hair until the cloth starts half way up them: sideways stripes of yellow-orange, green-pink, gold-blue, that circle more and more leg as they stretch and quiver on up. Her ringed thighs shake, they bounce. She jumps. Her belly rises as she hits the floor, floats up full, tied in a white sash, a big soft circle of cloth that could almost wish itself skin. But there are no wishes for the cloth, there are only its properties: color, weight and width. It's wound tight, with room for breath, around so much wild fatness, making its own song in motion, making a song in largeness. The fat and the sash ripple together, up with friction, down with passion. The woman moves herself all over, even her chin is shaking, even her fingers dart and wander, even her clothes are with her.

Notes

1 From Adrienne Rich, 'Women and Honour: Some Notes on Lying', *On Secrets and Silence: Selected Prose 1966–78*, WW Norton, New York, London, 1979.
2 The painting referred to is *Judith and Maidservant with the Head of Holofernes* by Artemisia Gentileschi.

Combat Gear
Sarah Harris

Naturally, it was black. Once, perhaps fifty years ago, it would have been worn only by a social butterfly, flitting from party to party. Pearly accessories – a clasp handbag, a new handkerchief, flesh-pink tights – would have set off the black stitching. It would have been beautiful.

But in 1981, it was just another dead woman's dress.

At fourteen, I found it in a charity shop, pressed up against stale-smelling, pale grey shirts and the crotch of a gentleman's pin-striped trousers. It was surrounded by one-legged Barbie dolls, a pile of children's Christmas annuals, and one out-of-service Action Man.

I could sense its original, hour-glass shape. But by 1981, its waistline had filled out. Flaring at the hips, its chest size had begun to shrivel. Its neck, still spat with a few, false pearls, rose matronly high. It had been let down so many times its hem had disappeared altogether; its skirt sank below the knees.

For this dress it had all, a long time ago, gone pear-shaped.

But I bought it. I paid for it, during my school lunch-hour, with pocket money that should have been spent at Miss Selfridge or Chelsea Girl. These were the shops my mother had in mind when she gave me that money. Shops haunted by girls all shades of pastel pink, their boyfriends standing bored by the electric doors.

'I'm home,' I grunted, dumping my quilted, blush-pink schoolbag by the front door.

'Did you buy anything?' my mother called from the kitchen.

I took out my new, antique dress, holding it up against me, in front of the full-length mirror in the hallway.

'Yes,' I said, defensively.

'What's it like?'

'It's *lovely*,' I called through, adding bitterly: 'So, of course, *you* won't like it.'

Up to my neck in that dress, no longer did my reflection say 'fourteen'. Instead, with the dress held there, in front of the mirror, I had grown into the sort of woman who wore silk dressing gowns, drinking black coffee at lunchtime. I was the woman in cafeterias, or feet up in her own flat, appearing in provocative photographs in the *New Musical Express* or *Sounds*, having spent all night queuing up outside cavernous night-clubs such as the Batcave. I had only to hang a filthy cigarette from my mouth to look like *her*, my image of the dangerous 1980s woman, swallowing vodka and knocking back drugs.

'Are you having supper?' my mother called through. 'Only you never eat a square meal any more. All I ask is that you eat some vegetables.'

'Oh, for God's sake, I've eaten,' I said, as she appeared in the hallway, dripping a dishcloth. 'Just stop interfering in my life.'

'That's not...?'

'What now?' I snapped.

'*Please*,' she said. 'Tell me that's *not* the dress you bought.'

Did my mother know that, with the dress held up to me, I had become the type of woman – her eyes circled in black eyeliner, face talcum-powder white, her mat of dyed black hair back-combed and sprayed stiff with hair lacquer – who lived her life at the core of the capital's Tube map? That, now, I wasn't just yet another suburban girl, pushed away from anything *London* and exciting, languishing at the end of the Metropolitan line?

'It's from a secondhand shop, isn't it?'

'Yes, but what that's got to do with it...'

'Why couldn't you buy something *fashionable*? Why couldn't you buy something *pretty*, like other girls your age?' she asked, sharpening her voice. 'Don't you want clothes that everyone else wears?'

I didn't want pretty. I certainly didn't want to be like everyone else. Had it not been for the dress, I would, that day, have been just another schoolgirl, fusing plugs in Physics, making peg-boxes in Arts and Crafts. Without it, folded inside a brown paper bag at the bottom of my schoolbag, I could have been any old fourteen-year-old on the Tube ride home, throwing pencil cases at boys.

For where, without it, was the difference? Travelling home from school through stations with stultifying names such as Pinner, North Harrow and Northwood Hills (any green bought in patches from the garden centre), I was just another uniform, living in just another square house, its outline so clear a child could have drawn it. (Coloured in sand-beige, my house was modestly parenthesised by grass; it had just enough garden to make the neighbours envious.

'It's *my* life. And it *is* what everyone's wearing,' I said.

'You mean it's what *Alice* is wearing.'

With such a dress, I could become my best friend, Alice, who subscribed to the *New Musical Express* rather than *Smash Hits*. She had painted her wallpaper black, dripping with song lyrics, graffitied in red; my own striped paper matched my school uniform, its pop-star posters stuck on by my Dad with Blu-Tack from Rymans. As the dominant colour in her wardrobe she had black; most of her clothes were that middle-of-the-night shade. By contrast, as was typical of any middle-class Metropolitan Line girl, my cupboard was stuffed full of candy-pinks and bottle-blues.

'You'll wear it out over my dead body,' threatened my

mother, returning to the kitchen.

'Yeah, yeah,' I said, bored.

'Over my *dead body*.'

I ignored her: like any other fourteen-year-old girl, I allowed my mother to have little bearing on my life. But deep down I knew that, with or without her approval, I could never wear that dress outside. In all honesty, I didn't dare to. Perhaps if I'd had the precocity of Kelly Parker (who fell pregnant at thirteen), Alice's permissive parents, or Dawn's elder brother, Duncan (*in* a band, *on* drugs), I might have worn it ice-skating, say, or to the local bowling alley. I might, at the very least, have worn it to an out-of-town shopping centre.

But for me – whose after-dark trips to London happened vicariously, and through the pages of music magazines – revolution wouldn't happen overnight. It was enough that evening to know that, hidden in a bag beneath Benetton jumpers and boxes of square-toed shoes, was a lived-in, *womanly*, black dress.

And to know that, the following morning, I would begin to iron out the box pleats in my school skirt.

Divestments

Carol Mara

It still happens although less often now. I am walking through the shopping centre and I see a pair of shorts or more usually a shirt. A brand name surf shirt, Billabong or Rusty or Quiksilver – the icons associated with Australian teenage identity; or something baggy; perhaps a cartoon character printed loudly on black cotton. And the response is immediately in my mind, 'William would like that'. Almost as suddenly as the unbidden thought has arisen my present rational mind sweeps it away. For William, my son, has been dead for three years now.

At thirteen William would have chosen such items of clothing; more likely I would have chosen them for him or it would be a joint collaboration. But at sixteen he might have grown to reject or abhor those more 'juvenile' fancies. I'll never know. I can only guess.

I remember the pleasure of choosing and buying clothes for all my children and recall the cold comfort it brought when my mother would bring them boxes of clothes with the rejoinder that 'You won't have to buy them anything this season.' And the winter when all the jumpers and overalls were dark grey or mouse-dun, the colour of ashes, reflecting the emotional pall over her own life.

Then I felt deprived of a pleasure, that once again she was in subtle control: that she would decide what my children wore.

It was at times like this that my adolescent battles over clothes would launch return raids into my consciousness. Of turning over the waistbands of skirts, two, three times after I had left the house, to bring the skirt above my knees; of the look and words of disapproval ('Isn't that weekend wear?') on the day I first wore jeans to lectures; of the bikini I was made to return to David Jones ('Just tell them it's unsuitable'); and of the words that stung and humiliated – 'And don't think you're going out of this house looking like that.'

'Like that' could have been anything: a scarf knotted around the neck; shoes that needed polishing; a hem slightly askew; a fine ladder on the inside of a stocking leg; colours that didn't 'match'. All attempts to control the expanding identity of her daughter.

What secret delinquency there was in going about the house without pants under a knee-length skirt; or tying a scarf gypsy style around my head and dancing around when no one else was at home.

My own children were, by eleven or twelve, developing their own tastes. With each purchase there was a dance of lobbying to persuade me to spend money accommodating their new and sometimes outlandish choices.

William had chosen the baggy black pants he was wearing the morning before he was killed. And the long man-sized blue shirt I had bought from The Reject Shop. Its origins hadn't worried him although the reason for its 'reject' status became patently and potently clear the first time he wore it: his torso and arms were coloured a bruised blue. I'd chilled at the sight of him, remembering only too clearly the six weeks he'd spent in hospital just months before. With two broken arms and a broken hip after falling from a tree, he had spent a first agonising week, both arms in plaster, his leg in traction after a metal plate and pin had been inserted, morphine dripping into his arm, lying naked under the sheet except for a flannelette patch tied across his genitals.

His nakedness had distressed him – his identity stripped

from his pubescent body, half man, half boy. I bought silky boxer pants and slit them down one side to fit around his pelvis and for above the waist he had requested that I apply wash-off tattoos a friend had brought in to him. I tattooed his chest and his shoulders and only baulked at the one displaying a skull and crossbones. 'Not that one Will, too close to the bone,' and we had both laughed.

He'd dressed with careful carelessness the day of the party, the day of his death. His long-sleeve Rip Curl shirt, his black and purple nylon surf shorts, his old daggy white joggers and not the newer cleaner ones I'd recently bought, and his old holey basketball socks, Chicago Bulls on the ribbing. I will never see the shorts or the shirt again. The shorts go as forensic evidence, the shirt I imagine cut from his body as he lay by the roadside.

One day, about nine months after his death, I get a phone call from a local police sergeant: what do I want done with his clothes? 'I want them,' I say. They are the objects which had last contact with his conscious living body.

When I go to collect them I have to wait in the foyer and eventually when the sergeant is free he goes to the safe and brings out a large crumpled blue garbage bag. He opens it to verify that the objects within are indeed those belonging to my son. I sign the book that says they are now in my possession.

At home I take out each object: his socks, one cut in half; his joggers, the soles still clutching the roadside gravel; one of his orthotics; his underpants which bear a black mark I become convinced is the place of first impact with the car that ran him down then drove away; his watch still keeping time and set seven minutes fast, the way he always liked it. I put them back into the bag and they remain in his bottom drawer with his Cub Scout uniform and his brown Doc Martens school shoes.

Another drawer contains the clothes I could not bear to

give away or throw out. The baggy black pants, the long blue shirt, his primary school jacket, his favourite winter top, his Tweety Bird T-shirt and five or six other articles that hold special significance or memory – all carefully and lovingly washed and ironed. There's also a pair of his underpants which he'd left lying on the floor, unwashed, inside a plastic bag, his own distinctive smell on them.

Some of his clothes we wear. His father wears his socks, his younger sister some of his shirts, waiting to grow into others. I wear his black Quiksilver sloppy joe, the one he'd waited patiently to wear, bought at a summer sale and put away till winter. So pleased and proud of it, he was.

That day when we are summoned urgently to the hospital he is once again naked on a hospital bed, no tattoos this time, his only adornment amid the mess of tubes and machinery a white bandage around his head seeping blood, his life ebbing away.

When the coroner finally releases his body we go to see him at the funeral chapel. They have dressed him and laid him in his coffin in a pale blue shroud. It fitted the moment and I could not have borne, then, to part with his favourite black pants and blue shirt, the most fitting graveclothes for a cool dude of thirteen.

I give his un-named school clothes to the school uniform pool; his younger male cousin wants his Kuta Lines jacket; I give other objects and photos to his friends, thinking they may be wary of wearing their dead friend's clothes; so many, over time, become bundled up and put into anonymous plastic bags and left in the charity bin at the shopping centre; and then there are those in the drawers that now carry an emotional power beyond any true worth of the pile of used fabric that in time they will become. Gradually, I know, I will divest the drawers of these clothes when they no longer hold the terrible potency that they assumed one Saturday in September. But not just yet.

The Red Dress
Helen Dunmore

Even when my mother had three children under six, she was one of these women who always manage to suggest the existence of the adult world to her daughters. Small children on a tight budget in the fifties must have been hard work physically. No fridge, so we walked to the shops daily, one in the pram, two trotting beside it. There were coal fires in sitting room and dining room, a coke boiler in the kitchen, a primitive washing-machine, and a vacuum cleaner which seemed to belch out more dust than it ingested. But I cannot remember my mother looking drab.

She was a slender woman, very pale-skinned, with clear blue eyes. She had married after taking degrees at Manchester and at Oxford, and kept the love of clothes she had developed in those years, as well as some of the clothes themselves. I can remember hiding myself in the folds of her New Look skirts, or fingering a beautiful creamy knitted-silk evening stole. My sister and I clopped up and down in our mother's high heels, wondering how we would ever learn to balance in them, or keep our stockings up with those mysteriously buttoned suspender belts. The greatest luxury was to get out her wedding dress of oyster satin, embroidered with pearls which we believed were real, and feel its chill slither on our own skin. The wedding dress disappeared in one of our many moves, but another dress remained: this was the red velvet dress.

It was always my favourite. My grandfather had given my

mother the velvet, which is a heavy, deep crimson, so dark that it has plum-coloured shadows in it. The dress was made up by a dressmaker who was skilled at copying designs from fashion magazines, either in 1949 or early 1950. The design is elegant but simple: a V neck at the back, a shallow scoop at the front, the cut following the lines of the body. There is a red velvet rose at the hip. It was one of my mother's most successful dresses: the dark rich colour brought out her fair skin. There was something sumptuous in the cloth. Children may not know whether their parents really are objectively beautiful or not, but they know when their parents feel beautiful. I could tell that in her red dress my mother felt beautiful, set apart, faintly glowing. Rosamond Lehmann in *The Weather in the Street*, describes that glow: 'Yes, all was well. For this evening some illusion was being breathed out, some reflection thrown back of a power as mystic, as capricious in its comings and goings as it was recognisable when it came.'

But the dress as it exists now, and the dress as it was made, are not the same. At some time skirts became shorter. My mother rashly decided that she would cut the dress to fit the fashion. I am sure she did it herself, judging from the long impatient stitches on the hem. And I'm equally sure that she regretted it. Not immediately perhaps, when the butchered dress fitted convention better than the original with its long, balanced line; but later, certainly.

A few years later, she stopped wearing the dress. The last times are so much harder to recognise and remember than the first. The first time a baby is put into your arms; who forgets that? But the last time you lift the heavy four or five-year-old isn't as easy to remember. Maybe the dress needed a stitch – the velvet rose is loose – and she couldn't be bothered to put one in. Or it needed cleaning but she never got around to it. And of course the body changes, the fit is not what it was. But the red dress continued to travel with her, from house to house. It had a hushed, musty smell but the colour still shone at the back of the cupboard where it hung inside-out.

I've always wanted to resurrect it. It's old now, frankly old, whitened at the seams, the rose hanging, the zip broken. There is a tear along a side-seam. It looks as if some animal has been at it, during those long years in the dark. The velvet hasn't stiffened, though: it is still supple, like skin, even though the fabric is impregnated with dust.

What a pity it is cut short. If only it still made that beautiful narrow curve from hip to mid-calf. I find myself wondering what became of the band of fabric my mother sheared off and threw away. I expect we played with it, or made plump, peony-red pincushions stuffed with the sheep's wool which we found on barbed wire. I remember being taught at school that the grease in the wool would prevent the pins from rusting.

I have the red dress in my wardrobe now. It is so battered that if I saw it in a secondhand shop I would pass over it. But there is still something there. When I hold it up to the light there is still the colour, and the dense nap of the velvet. It must be steam-cleaned, and the rose must be stitched back. What looks at first glance like a jagged, gaping tear can be folded back and resewn along the seam. And the hem, so poorly made, can be remade. The dress is older than I am; can an illusion be remade, too? And can an object of desire be transferred from one owner to another without losing its vital magic?

Another solution has occurred to me. I could take the red dress to a dressmaker who would be able to use it as a pattern. Fresh velvet, an unfaded colour, the dress reborn in its original length and style. It could be done. But I am not so sure that I will be able to find a bolt of velvet to match the one chosen by the expert eye of my grandfather, or a dressmaker to spread it out, a pool of crimson in the grey of postwar austerity.

*

It is 1949. The dressmaker runs her hand over the velvet, with the nap. She turns, measures and pins, marks the cloth with tailor's chalk, and then poises her scissors to cut that exact, definitive line.

Freudian Slips and Blue Jeans

Sarah Dreher

The other day, when my therapist came to greet me in her waiting room, I noticed her checking out my clothes.

I knew I looked like something you'd find on the floor of a laundromat. When I'd left the house – in a rush and too early in order not to be too late – I found it was colder than I'd expected. No telling where my winter clothes were, I never find them before February. So I grabbed the first thing I saw lying around. (You can always find lots of things to wear lying around at my house if you don't care what you look like.) It turned out to be a blue-and-white horizontally striped hooded flannel jacket. It clashed, not quite jauntily, with my blue-and-gold vertically striped shirt.

'I know what you're thinking,' I began, embarrassed and self-conscious and a little defensive, 'they don't match, but…' Better to let them know *you know* you are screwed up, if you know what I mean.

'Actually,' she replied, 'I was wondering why you're not wearing a warmer coat.'

Trying to read your therapist's mind and getting it wrong plus realizing she probably thinks you're passively suicidal and trying to invent a life-threatening illness…well it's an ugly way to start the day.

But that's how it is with clothes and me. Always trouble.

I have two pictures of myself, taken when I was twelve years old. In the first, I'm wearing my great-grandmother's green and pink brocade off-the-shoulder wedding dress. I'm seated in a studio, gazing languidly into the distance, one arm draped gracefully across a table. Waiting for my prince to come, I guess. It was my mother's favorite picture. She kept it on the piano in the living room to serve as an inspiration.

In the other I'm wearing baggy shorts, a shirt two sizes too large, and brown Oxfords. Limp socks, skinned knee, and probably worms in my shirt pocket. I'm looking directly into the camera, laughing, one arm draped around my best friend's shoulders. Between us we're holding a large dead fish on a stringer. I have no idea who took the picture. Certainly not my mother. This was my favorite picture of me. I kept it hidden.

I've always had an uneasy relationship with my clothes. For one thing I have the kind of skin that's so sensitive I can count the stitches in my socks through the bottoms of my feet. Add to that the joys of coming of age in the 1950s — that heyday of stiff taffeta, starched crinolines, girdles and garter belts, and long-line bras with bonestays.

And, just for fun, throw in a mother who was obsessed with me being 'feminine' (Gee, do you think she suspected something?) 'Feminine' meant frills, lace, puffy, and one size too small. In my teen years, we argued constantly about my clothes. 'I can't believe you're wearing *that* filthy thing,' was her standard comment.

For a while that confused me, as I was rather fastidious as a child (except for the worms in the pocket, of course). But, as I grew older and wiser and more experienced in the ways of the world, I realized that for her 'filthy' was a synonym for 'butch'.

In my family's home, we dressed for holidays. Now, not only are holidays abstractions, and not inclined to notice how you're dressed, but I was taught that holidays were a time of mandatory delight, whether you felt like it or not. I was supposed to 'enjoy myself'. And everyone else.

Picture it. I'm at a festive party, my feet stuffed into high heels which tilt me forward at an anxiety-producing angle. My nylons make my feet clammy and hold the moisture against my skin. I'm starting to itch between the toes. My half-slip doesn't cover my midriff, which leaves my skin in direct contact with the underside of my wool dress. I'd considered a full slip, but didn't want to worry all night about the straps showing. My bra, also strapless, is hard wired and very perky. The kind of thing Madonna would slip into for outerwear. When I look down, I can see bosoms. It's just that they don't look like *my* bosoms. My hair feels starched, my required 'perm' flat on the top of my head but bursting into frizz at shoulder height. My lipsticked lips feel as if I've been sucking paraffin. I'm supposed to scan myself in the nearest available mirror every few minutes to make sure Everything Is In Place. I am expected to 'sparkle'.

And may you have a Happy New Year, too.

I rebelled, in my own way. At boarding school, I spent an inordinate amount of time working backstage on theater productions. It was fun. It got you out of church the day following a production. And you were supposed to wear jeans. I chose my college partially because 'girls' were allowed to wear slacks, shorts, and jeans there.

In graduate school, and for a while afterward as a practising clinical psychologist and college teacher, I dressed in a 'professional manner'. Heels and hose, and tailored dresses. The tailored dresses were a compromise. Mother would have preferred more frills. In the early 1960s, you also wore slips. Nylon slips. I was living in the Midwest. There is no thrill like that of feeling the winter wind — a gale of -5° Fahrenheit blowing down from the Rockies and across 1000 miles of frozen earth — toss your nylon slip against your nylon-wrapped legs. Think razor blades.

Then, at last, the Women's Liberation Movement came

along and liberated me from my wardrobe.

We did a lot of talking about clothes, inside and outside of Consciousness Raising groups. The Women's Movement required a great deal of talking. No Liberation without Conversation. We agonized over the politics, the economics, 'fashion' as a class issue. In case you missed it, the fashion industry fuels its Patriarchal Corporate Profits by keeping us uncomfortable with ourselves in uncomfortable clothes in which it is impossible to relax, have a good time, or escape a rapist. At the same time, it separates us from our sisters by class (who has the 'better', more expensive clothes?)

The solution, we knew, was to adopt the universal uniform of Revolution – jeans, blue work shirts, and boots.

One day in October 1972, I wore a dress for the last time. I have a friend who first met me on that very day. Every year on that date we meet to pay homage to our mutual liberation.

Needless to say, we've lost a good bit of our zeal for revolutionary *haute couture*. Plus the clothing manufacturers have gotten into the act, and now there are jeans we can't afford, and it's fashionable to wear them almost everywhere.

And we still have 'Victoria's Secret' perched on the doorstep like a stray virus waiting for a chance to sneak in.

Ah, yes, my friends, dress codes are coming back, and it's not a lovely sight.

As for myself, I pretty much please myself these days. I figure I've paid my dues. If what I wear isn't always entirely appropriate... well, I've earned a reputation for being peculiar that does nicely as an excuse.

Which is *not* to say my wardrobe and I are living happily ever after. You don't experience years of sarcasm and disgust and abuse, and one morning just say, 'Wow! Mom was wrong!' and get on with your life. After all, I can still reach down and find some disapproval to project on to my therapist. But I'm better at dressing in ways that express me.

For a reading or a talk, for instance, I try to wear something loose and soft and kind of special looking. The message is, 'I'm not scary and I'm glad to be here.'

When I'm doing psychic work, I go for something exotic or at least odd. I think Spirit is more impressed with oddity.

Camping almost anything goes, as long as it has pockets. Ditto for writing. No fuss, no muss, don't bother me.

For seeing clients, I exchange the T-shirt for a real shirt, and the hiking boots for sneakers as a sign of respect and serious intent. That's a compromise, too. My idea of Truly Serious Intent is that revolutionary uniform. It says we're here to work.

At my father's funeral, I wore black jeans, hiking boots, a red corduroy shirt, and mirrored aviator sunglasses. It wasn't exactly a fashion statement, but it was a statement.

I haven't decided yet what I want to be buried in.

Maybe my great-grandmother's wedding dress?

a girl who likes sex best
when clothes are on
bell hooks

Clothes exist not simply to cover the body but to celebrate it as well. That's why adornment, why fashion and style, play such a vital role in the lives of people everywhere in the world, no matter how poor or 'underdeveloped'. The body as a human temple is always present, and garments always needed to shield and shelter this sanctuary. To me clothes always express an erotic aesthetic. I like clothing that is divinely sensual. Clothing that adorns and caresses my flesh. It is widely known by all my devout readers that I enjoy wearing fine lingerie. And think undergarments are especially important – my closets have baskets filled with luscious silks, linen, and lace. However, it is quite easy to find luxurious and beautiful lingerie especi- ally if clothes are essential to your erotic pleasure – that is if you are a girl who likes sex best when clothes are on and not off. Now if they come off in the process that's cool and it means merely that the sensual pleasure has been taken to another level.

Any woman who is into sex and clothes is usually into fabrics. Those of us who are not into the dominatrix aesthetics of sticky leather, slick vinyl and wet plastic look on the more natural, ecological, fibers to enhance our sexual pleasure – hence the lust for silks, fine cottons, handkerchief soft linen and the sweet softness of finely spun cashmere. I like to imagine that the recent craze for velvet in both outerwear and underwear is a sex thing.

At the close of an intense discussion about vernacular

architecture with a new man, or should I say, another man in my life, I noticed that he was staring at the crystal buttons on my deep crimson velvet shirt. I had been reading to him the line in Bernard Tschumi's *Architecture and Disjunction* where he writes: 'Unlike the necessity of mere building, the non-necessity of architecture is indissociable from architectural histories, theories, and other precedents. These bonds enhance pleasure. The most excessive passion is always methodical. In such moments of intense desire, organization invades pleasure to such an extent that it is not always possible to distinguish the organizing constraints from the erotic matter.' We were discussing the way certain buildings have an organic sensuality.

Since he was staring so at the shirt, I invited him to touch the fabric with his hands – to feel the texture. Momentarily I had forgotten I was braless – that when he ran his hands over the fiber he would also be touching my breasts and possibly arousing me. And there were my nipples growing hard for hands caressing velvet, and it occurred to me that there was no reason to stop there; that it would be useful to explore further, to taste the feel of a hungry mouth sucking breasts through velvet (we were both ravenous and about to get dinner). The feel of wet velvet against skin is quite enticing, certainly a stimulant to the appetite. Our book had unwittingly been left open at the page with a picture of a poster which declares: 'Sensuality has been known to overcome even the most rational of buildings. Archictecture is the ultimate erotic act. Carry it to excess and it will reveal both the traces of reason and the sensual experience of space. Simultaneously.'

When I see women running around in velvet I often wonder about the nature of their sexual experiences – if the feel of fabric is important to the fulfillment of desire or if it's just a sensual allure. For me clothing is never solely a sensual allure, or mere prop; it is always an essential aspect of sexual experience. Perhaps it's some carry-over from the days of old-fashioned adolescence where all sexual longings had to be expressed with clothes on. In our house, full of girls (I have five sisters), there was always someone present to be a 'spy in the house of love'. Hence it was a necessary, though daring, act to find ways of exploring sexual feelings with one's clothes on.

Finding lingerie that is sensual is a much easier task than finding clothes that give the body a constant erotic thrill. To me cashmere is one of the most resilient and fun fibers. I discovered the full intensity of its erotic powers and pleasures quite by accident. I had awakened on my birthday confident that I was too old for the joys of illicit pleasure – certain that it was no fun to be involved with someone who was not free to awaken you and celebrate the day, so I was determined to end this love affair, the most compelling romantic bond of my entire life. I dressed quickly, throwing clothes into a small black bag with no thought. They would all match because everything was black. It's my favorite color – an urban New York thing – a woman thing. In the memoir of my girlhood, *Bone Black*, I wrote about longing to wear black as a child and being told by my mother that I could not, because it was not for just anyone – for innocent girls – that one had to earn the right to wear black – that 'black is a woman's color'. Forever after, the color black was intimately linked in my mind with emotional experience, maturity, and the knowledge of intense passion, particularly the pain of loss.

Since it was early fall everything thrown into the small black bag had to be warm; it was the perfect moment for cashmere. I threw in a long black cashmere skirt with matching jumper – clothes I wear to work whether in the office or at home. While I did not think my journey was leading to erotic passion, I choose sweaters with buttons. To me, buttons are always great for sensual play, because they open up the possibility of pleasure. Yet when I was decisively throwing clothes into my black bag to catch a plane and travel thousands of miles, sex was not on my mind. All I could think about was breaking the hold this relationship had on my heart.

I arrived on a dreary grey cold day – the heat in the small flat keeping it warm but not yet hot enough to break the chill. He did not know I was coming yet there was no expression of surprise that I showed up and wanted to talk. He knew by the sound of my voice as we discussed small things – the weather, a time to meet, etc. He had what the poet calls the 'sense of an ending'. Before he came I took a bath, filling the small rooms with odors of eucalyptus and lavender. Ready for warmth and serious conversation I donned my black skirt and sweater, an outfit normally worn to work – slightly formal but not strict. Only now I wore nothing underneath. Shrouded in soft cashmere I felt consoled, comforted yet still resolute.

When he walked through the door, I calmly shared that we needed to stop seeing one another. It was a calm rational farewell. We were like characters in a film, reading a carefully constructed script – dispassionate and clear. Yet when we held each other, our bodies hot in a hot room filled with the intensity of impending loss, we entered the realm of the senses. Pressed up against the wall near the door I could feel the coldness of the outside coming through my clothes and the heat coming from his touch as he caressed my body through soft cashmere. As his fingers entered my crotch through the skirt I was overwhelmed – it was wet and sensuous. Ours was a sweet leavetaking full of yearning and the sadness of loss.

That night changed my thinking about clothes I wear for everyday work. Suddenly I saw the cashmere clothes I wear for pure practicality in a new light. Now I see an elemental allure in these sturdy sweaters and skirts – an allure that like the remembered passion of true love lingers and sustains.

Glad Rags

Susie Boyt

I was an awkward nine year old, quite unsure of my place in the world. I knew I was rather important, that I had a way about me that was a bit heroic or stylish or unusual, but I had no idea how to communicate this to the other people in my life. I was an ungainly little person. I had the biggest feet in the class and an enormous appetite – once famously out-eating the husband of my mother's best friend, a gentle giant of six foot seven. Consequently I did not cut a dainty figure in the classroom. Yet despite this, I knew all I needed was to find my own way of shining and then all would be well.

About this time I started attending dancing classes. These were conducted in a local church hall by a formidable matron we knew as Miss Audrey. Monday was tap, for which we wore a red leotard with a shallow pleated skirt attached. Tuesday was 'modern' a type of dance that involved lots of saucy grinning and high kicks, and Wednesday was ballet for which we wore pale blue Royal Academy of Dancing leotards with narrow flesh coloured elasticated belts. While we obeyed Miss Audrey's commands, beginning and ending each lesson with a prima ballerina curtsey to the floor ('Thank you very much Miss Audrey' 'Thank you very much little girls'), our mothers sat round the edge of the room on brown stacking chairs, smoking furiously. The more devoted amongst them had memorised the steps of our routines and tried to communicate them telepathically to their daughters: 'hop shuffle hop brush step brush step, step ball change pick up toe hop, hop shuffle hop brush step brush step, brush hop step step step brush hop... come on... you can do it... don't forget to smile... that's right, that's right.

Shortly after this I began to conceive an interest in two of the girls in the class above. One, a tall, slender English girl called Sarah Holmes, attended Miss Audrey's classes in the subdued green uniform of the Arts Educational School. I knew little about this school apart from the fact that at two o'clock every day, the ordinary lessons (English, French History) undertaken in the morning were eschewed for ballet, movement and voice classes. What really impressed me was that to mark this shift of gear from the academic to the theatrical, the pale bluey green nylon headband of the morning had to be changed for a deeper turquoise one. This was actually a school rule. The headbands were to be purchased at Freeds of London in St Martin's Lane and although I was not a pupil at the school I began observing this practice also.

The other girl who caught my eye was a glamorous South American girl with thick curly black hair, who was called Zany. Her appoach was less dignified than that of Sarah Holmes, but equally alluring. She was more showbiz, and I had seen her practising for a dancing festival in silver top hat and diamanté-trim leotard. Zany attended the Italia Conte stage school in London and sported its smart royal blue blazer and impossibly chic, light blue and mid-blue hound'stooth-checked kilt. 'Give 'em the ol' razzle dazzle' was the song and dance number she performed in our Christmas extravaganza which took place in Hackney Town Hall, her body compact and dazzling in slinky catsuit complete with stick on sequins and silver Oxfords customized with Capezio American teletone taps.

Then, one Sunday afternoon, I saw a documentary on

television on the Italia Conte stage school in which Bonnie Langford and Lena Zavaroni, all fishnets and ringlets, closed the show with, 'It's not where you start it's where you finish.' As they threw their hats in the air and sang their hearts out, shuffling off to Buffalo and jigging their open palms from side to side, I thought, that's it. It was then that I broached the matter with my mother.

My mother has always allowed me to do as I wished in life but on this one occasion she put her foot down hard. Perhaps she sensed my rounded form and inquiring mind would be out of place at stage school. Maybe she envisaged me as the chubby girl in Grange Hill or some other kiddy TV show, being teased by my cruel classmates. It's not impossible that the thought of spending every weekend driving around to castings for adverts and voice-overs filled her with dread. Or was it the prospect of Bonnie Langford coming round to our house for tea?

I did have some genuine dancing talent and a sweet singing voice and the more I thought about it, the more going to stage school seemed the obvious next move in my chosen career path. I explained to my mother that if my general talent for light entertainment went undeveloped it would not only be a tragedy, we would be acting in a manner that was wildly irresponsible. I read her the parable of the talents and stepped up my campaign to make her change her mind. I perfected my tap routines in a dinner jacket bought at Oxfam and a trilby, as worn by Judy Garland to sing 'Forget Your Troubles, Come on Get Happy', and danced along to my Fred Astaire records. I started walking round the major parks of London dressed in red gingham and singing show tunes quite loudly in the hope that a holidaying casting director, out for a stroll, say, would glimpse me and leap at the chance of signing me up. I often spoke of being signed up, without knowing exactly what it would mean apart from a welcome surfeit of glitter and sequins. I practised my audition pieces and sewed pink and lilac lazy daisies on to a bottle green Viyella shirtwaister that I thought would make suitable interview attire. We were locked in a full scale war of wills, but still my mother would not back down. The date for application drew near and then passed. I still insisted that it was not too early to apply for the following year, but my pleas fell on deaf ears.

Then, the night before my birthday, my mother came into my bedroom with an early package for me. 'I know that if you went to Italia Conte you would be really unhappy,' she said and although she had said it to me fifty times before, suddenly I felt she could see something vulnerable in me that she wanted to protect. She continued and I half listened. It wouldn't be chorus girls in the dinner queue and everyone bursting into song at the drop of a hat. There wouldn't be the austere but highly gifted Russian ballet teachers who were hard as nails until the perfection of your arabesque melted their hearts, like the ones I had read about in Noel Streatfield's books. 'It would be much harder than that, some of the people would be really competitive and nasty, and... and critical...' she added. It wouldn't be like Miss Audrey's at all. They'd try and make me into something I wasn't, apparently. Make me wear loads of orange make-up, force me to sing in an American accent. Put me on a starvation diet. They might even have communal weigh-ins. At this news I sat bolt upright in bed.

'Weigh-ins, really?' I said trying to sound as casual as possible. 'What, at the beginning of each term?'

'It might even be every week. Of course I don't know for sure. Anyway I bought you this as a compromise.'

I opened the gift slowly and beneath the four layers of sugar-almond-pink tissue paper, I saw a scrap of light blue and mid-blue hound's-tooth checked fabric. It was the skirt of the Italia Conte school that I had admired on Zany, and fancied myself in more than once. I leapt up and tried it on. Even though it was teamed with a Minnie Mouse nightie, I felt it usher in a whole new world of glamour and sophistication. I put on my tap shoes and tried a shuffle hop step in it in front of the mirror. The pleats at the back were knife edge sharp and the whole garment was very stiff. I smoothed down the flap at the front. It looked wonderful.

'I am sorry. I know it's not really, I know it's not really the same as – ' My mother's voice trailed off nervously. She did not know how I was going to react. I nodded with her in agreement. It wasn't the same. It wasn't the same at all. But it was pretty good...

Clothes Have No Memory
Beverly Pagram

We fought over it, the lace dress. I'd seen it first, you see, in the window of the charity shop. Looking for all the world like black ice ferns sewn together, it trailed forlornly over an old-fashioned dressmaker's dummy in between a basket of corsets and a mound of sad handbags.

'I'm having that,' I announced briskly as we went into the fug of the shop from the sleety street.

Fluorescent lighting and walls covered in aluminium baking-foil certainly didn't do the clientele or the clothes any favours at the used goods emporium belonging to the Little Sisters of Perpetual Redemption. The scruffy, shuffling masses seemed pale and luminous as if they had just arrived from a distant, depressed planet. The donated clothes and accessories – the usual mix of dodgy nylon wigs, vast nylon housecoats and Polynesian-themed shirts, lay about unappealingly in the irradiating dazzle. Over this alien scene presided Mrs Zolinda, a minute Armenian lady who wore a towering bun and many religious amulets. She fancied herself as a sort of nun-by-proxy, and on many of our previous visits searching for elusive sumptuous stuffs among the acrylic cardies, scuffed boots and plates of tangled beads like mournful eyeballs, she dropped to the ground in prayer without warning.

'Mrs Zolinda has fainted!' you cried the first time this happened, ferreting about for the vanished manageress in the swivelling islands of musty ex-nursing home daywear. Located by a barrage of Hail Marys issuing mysteriously from behind an ankle-length chenille garment, Mrs Zolinda finished her orisons by petitioning the Almighty that 'this nice two gels finds zomesing verry nice right now,' and making an extravagant sign of the cross with a rosaried claw-hand.

Strangely enough we almost always did. Assorted acts of grace allowed us to find a crystalline diamanté necklace in the pocket of a plastic mac; a 1940s crêpe blouse with tiny shimmering buttons; a wonderfully sleazy tit-revealing jumper in mauve mohair; a flared skirt emboldened with cobalt-blue tulips; a shellwork brooch in the shape of a ship. Usually we shared these finds out equably and affably, taking it in turns when we both spotted the same treasure at the same time. Not on this occasion, however.

I went to Mrs Zolinda's counter, with its stern sign 'IN THE INTERESTING OF HIGENICS PLEASE KEEP ON YOUR PANTS! IN THE CHANGE ROOM' to ask her to take the black lace dress out of the window. Unfortunately she was irritably busy, wrapping some beige acrylic trews and a copy of 'Karmic Kooking' for a leather-skinned gent wearing a flight bag from a long-defunct airline across his chest-exposing shirt. It was then that you appeared breathlessly behind me, with the gossamer black dress over your arm, if you please.

'I climbed in the window to get it. I'm having it. I know it's your turn. I'm sorry. I've got to have it!' you whispered stridently, fixing me with a baleful glare.

'Pardon me?'

'I said I'm having it!' Your eyes glittered dangerously, your skin was damp and pale. 'I *need* it!'

Mrs Zolinda attempted to lighten the ensuing insufferable silence by calling on us to remember the unbeatable generosity of Our Lord and offering me *gratis*, by way of compensation, a mother-of-pearl and cork bark diorama of the shrine at Lourdes, bearing the entreaty: MARY SAVE US. I regret to say it was refused ungraciously.

When we got outside the shop the weather had cleare
sky a pellucid pale grey. I continued my sulk as we waite
the bus, and you unwisely prattled on about your
purchase. It was in a dream last week, you related, that yo
seen this actual black papery dress, so when you saw it in t
charity shop you just had to have it.

'You said yourself that the reason we go to charity shops to
buy our clothes is not just for reasons of economy, but because
the older things have unknown past lives, secret histories…

'Bullshit,' I said. 'They're just dead ladies' draperies. Clothes
have no memory. You just wanted that atticky old frock
because you thought it looked rather special and it gives you
exquisite pleasure not to let me have it.'

I told her the dress almost certainly wouldn't fit over her big
bum cheeks. That it looked like a pile of flies in a coma.

'Anyway. Who was wearing it in your dream? The Princess
of Darkness?'

'Just a woman,' you muttered. 'I couldn't see her face. Only
her back.'

Dream schmeam, I thought later that night when just to
annoy me you wore the dress to the pub. Even teamed
incongruously with a denim jacket there was no denying that
it looked fabulous. The voluminous shadowy lace skirt swirled
and eddied about, momentarily shrouding seated imbibers in a
nocturnal fog. The sleeves were long filigree tubes, the
architecture of the bodice a poem of intricate web-like
stitchery. Sly smiles of triumph were forthcoming from your
direction.

For a while you wore it constantly, usually in incongruous
settings like parks, supermarkets and inconsequential mid-
summer parties, where its glamorous dark presence always
drew confused and/or admiring glances. Then one day it got

...delicate veining of the lace shockingly wounded, its
...gly surprised criss-cross edges smeared with dank
...om the elder twigs that had rent them asunder.

...'t wear it now. It's spoiled. The magic's gone.'

...be daft. Take it to one of those Invisible Menders
...aid. 'It'll be as good as new.'

...rse I knew that this wasn't true, and gradually I grew
...ot seeing that frock at all. We went back to Mrs
...and bought a consolation skirt in rippling pleated
...k, with only the tiniest scorch mark near the waistband.

...o tell you the truth I was getting fed up with that dress,'
...confided. 'I handwashed it carefully several times but I
...ould never get rid of its strange odour.'

'Odour? Of what?'

'Oh, the usual charity shop pong…plus something else in
the background.'

'What exactly?' I asked. In fact I knew exactly what she
meant because I had occasionally caught a whiff of this near
undetectable scent myself.

Well… it's a bit musky like patchouli, a bit like cats, a bit like
damp earth… a bit like the inside of a very, very old wardrobe.
Really, it smells of HER. And that puts me off.'

I assumed that the dress had long since gone out with the
rubbish, in fact had almost forgotten its existence, when your
sudden death put me in the position of desolate archaeologist,
conservator and chucker-outer of some of your more
ephemeral effects. Drifting between shadowy, sparsely
furnished rooms I felt drawn to a trunk in the corner. It was
full of fabrics, mostly badly spotted with damp and hosting
silverfish. Underneath the vivid violet-blue dragon silk, a gift
from Beijing, lay a black rag – the tight frenzied loops of its
lace forced into droopy fish-scale shapes by the depradations of
countless moth children. It was really just an idea of a dress

now... a neckband, waistband, hem and cuffs just joined by confused tightropes of cotton. There was just one strip undamaged, and with a snip of scissors I freed it for ever.

I wear it as a scarf occasionally. Sometimes it seems completely non-perfumatory. On other occasions the sweet-sour aromatics it exudes are almost overpowering. Remembering what you said about the Dress Woman, I wonder if it is her I am smelling, or you, or both. All I know is that bits of the scarf unravel when I'm out walking, and disappear into the clear, bright air.

Free Dressing

Kate Cann

I wasn't at all sure I wanted to be included in an anthology about clothes. I mean – it's a bit of a soft subject, isn't it? Passive. Unimportant. And oddly terrifying. Wearing the right stuff can make you feel great about yourself, but you've got to *find* the right stuff first – you've got to *choose* it. And that's scary.

Everyone knows about shopaholics. Sad women who compulsively buy clothes to fill an aching emptiness in their lives. Once they've admitted they have a problem they can get therapy and help to come to terms with it. Where can I get help? I have the opposite problem, just as debilitating in its way. I'm a shop-phobic. I *can't* buy clothes. I come over all shaky and 'Oh, I can't be bothered' when I'm faced with a rack of trousers. I still feel proud of a posh coat I made myself buy four years ago, when I realised I had nothing but an anorak to wear to a christening – proud in the way you are when you've achieved something exceptional in your life. The trouble is it's four years old now and not so posh any more and – oh, God. I need to buy another one.

Too long in Marks & Spencer, and I get this terrible throat seizing panic, this existential rage, this desire to scream 'get a life!' at the women mooching through the underwear section. But I'm the one who should get a life. I just can't do it, I can't buy clothes. Why is it pleasurable for so many women – how can they think it's soothing? You're going to be wearing something that says 'I spent money on this. This is what I think looks good.' You're going to be *judged*. You might look like someone who cares too much about her appearance. You might look like someone who tries too hard. If you pull it off fine, but if you don't it's a disaster! It's blazoning out the message, 'I *really* thought about this and I still look like *shite!*'

That's why I'm so fond of wearing cast-offs. It's okay to look like shite in cast-offs because that's what they're all about. There's no real decision involved in their acquisition; they're about recycling, convenience, avoiding brain-numbing trips round the shops and saving money, not looking good. The other day I realised the only things I had on that I'd bought for myself was my underwear. Shirt and jeans chucked out by husband; belt someone left behind after an overnight visit; Doc Martens outgrown by daughter; socks stolen from son. Oddly enough, I didn't look that bad – maybe because everyone else's clothes are better than mine.

One of the problems with cast-offs, though, is letting people know that that's what they are. After all, you don't want them thinking you paid *money* for the tat you have on. That's one of the reasons I like freebie sweatshirts with some kind of printing (*Euro-Tour '96 – Sweden, Denver, Stockport*) that proves they were giveaways. I see them as the polar opposite of prominently named designer gear that screams 'I've been taken for a ride!' These sweatshirts proclaim that they were free, and it doesn't matter how crap they look, because they have a kind of moral superiority to make up for it. Which they do need, because they do look like crap. Even I only wear them for running in and walking the dog.

You mustn't think I don't care at all how I look. I do. I was a bit of a babe in the 1970s – well, I would have been, if the term had been invented then. But then, in my group, it was all down to hair and face and well – jeans, and little tops. Making an effort was naff in the extreme. I guess I'm still infected by all that. I hate dressing up. The last time I dressed up and wore heels

I felt like a man in drag – no, a man in drag who didn't want to be in drag. There's a big difference, or I imagine there is.

I do quite like men's clothes. I read recently that large women (which I am) look good in men's clothes (which I do sometimes) and I felt this gave a kind of seal of approval to my cross-dressing tendencies. This is useful because it means I can inherit and appropriate lots of my husband's gear, thus catering for two of my clothes fixations – masculine and cast-off – in one go. My four favourite waistcoats, though, I got new. I have this extraordinary, Southern-states father-in-law who sends huge boxes of presents over every Christmas, most of it ordered from TV shopping channels. Three Christmases running my husband got suede waistcoats. The first one was brown and it arrived when suede waistcoats were making a brief, fashionable appearance in the shops, and they cost an arm and a leg. I wouldn't have even considered forking out for one, but to be given one – okay, to steal one – was different.

It wasn't that hard to steal. My husband implied that he'd have all his teeth knocked out with a hammer before he even tried it on. I wore it over a loose white shirt and black jeans, and it looked great. I was the exact same colours as a cocker spaniel I'd once owned. The next day I put it on with two amber rings and amber earrings and went to a lunch party where another woman was also in a tan suede waistcoat. This didn't annoy me – far from it. I had fun smirking while she bemoaned the cost of her waistcoat and then even greater fun telling her I'd got mine for free. Next Christmas, a second waistcoat arrived. I hadn't told father-in-law the fate of the last one, just in case more were forthcoming. He hates me and adores his son (part of the fun is wearing something that would really piss him off if he knew about it). This one was wine-coloured – very seasonal, wonderful for not showing mulled wine spills.

The year after that, two more arrived. Another tan one,

which meant I could downgrade the other for everyday wear, and a cream one that looks dead posh partly because it's such an impractical colour. I wear it with antique Indian earrings like little incense shakers that are exactly the same creamy ivory colour as the suede. The waistcoat's looking less posh now it has grubby marks on it, but one of the great things about suede is that it ages so well. I feel a strong kinship with something that only improves the older and more worn it gets.

My four waistcoats are the backbone of my wardrobe. I can bung one on over jeans and a shirt and go just about anywhere. Lunch, party, theatre, meetings, anywhere. Team them up with the right earrings (I have no problem buying earrings), and you even look like you've made an effort. I don't care that they're not fashionable any more and may even in some way embody the spirit of naffness. They're just too effortless to give up. And they suit me. They tell people I'm a bit of a cross-dresser, a bit arty, a tad alternative and if I can get it in quickly that I didn't pay for them either, the telegraphing is complete. 'Hi! I'm Kate, and I stole this waistcoat. How many hours that could have been spent in various life-affirming activities did you spend shopping to get *that*?'

The Dress
Patricia Duncker

The Dress
of tapestries
and old mythologies
gives you fool's eyes,
helps you see the world
not as it could be, but as it is.

The Dress
isn't cotton
silk or velvet,
but man–made fibres,
100% acrylic, slimy to touch
and it smells if you sweat.

The Dress
doesn't fit,
is too short,
pinches my tits,
enlarges my bum,
makes me look stupid.

The Dress
isn't mine.
I borrowed it
tried it out,
wore it for years,
let out the bust – and the waist.

The Dress
is worn
by other women.
They look great,
sexy, voluptuous,
desirable, crazed, caged.

I've thrown out The Dress
I couldn't take it.
There's more enterprise
In walking naked.

The Pink Velvet Dressing Gown
Bulbul Sharma

Nobody is sure when the dressing gown first came into the family. I always thought that it belonged to my grandmother but my mother said it was her eldest aunt's – a present from her nephew, a black sheep who had emigrated to Canada and married a blond woman five years older than him. The aunt never wore it because she was sure the 'mem' had chosen it. Moreover it was a lurid shade of pink and her husband thought it would make her look like a woman of the bazaar. 'Which bazaar woman ever wears a dressing gown,' said my mother's aunt and my mother wondered how my uncle knew about such things.

After keeping it wrapped in its original gold embossed white plastic bag for a year, the aunt finally gave the dressing gown to my mother.

'What a stupid gift to send. She could never have worn it. The nephew must have gone mad after marrying that woman,' my mother grumbled every time she saw the dressing gown. The aunt, an energetic eighty-year-old lady could have never worn any dressing gown because women of her generation went to bed fully dressed in a sari, blouse and petticoat and only undressed while bathing. My mother never really used the dressing gown either, only wearing it on special occasions when unexpected visitors dropped by early in the morning before she had had her bath.

The dressing gown had a frilled collar edged with gold lace

and as the years went by the cruel Indian heat began to affect the velvet fabric, making it shrivel up around the edges. But the collar still held itself upright like a chameleon's ruffle, around my mother's cascading grey curls. My father said it made her look like Louis XIV, especially when she stood on the balcony quarrelling and bargaining with the vegetable hawker below on the street. Beggars passing by would often call out to her, 'O Queen, throw us a coin.' She tried to give the gown away to various relatives who came to visit but nobody would have it even though it was 'imported' and quite expensive. Years passed and the dressing gown began to look different. The soft pink gradually acquired a brownish glow like Europeans who have lived under the Indian sun for many years. The pink velvet changed its soft texture as patches of coconut hair oil, sandalwood talcum powder and Tiger 'headache' balm stained it with a pale gold patina, and the golden lace turned coppery with age.

Finally mother gave the dressing gown to me when I was in hospital having my first child. 'You can wrap the baby in it if it is a girl.' My mother-in-law did not want me to wear the dressing gown because she was worried it would tempt the Gods to send us a female child instead of the much longed for son. When my daughter was born I did not wrap her in the dressing gown because she was underweight and had to be kept inside an incubator. My mother knitted her a tiny pink blanket overnight and we would watch her through the glass panes as she slept curled up like a pink caterpillar. I wore the dressing gown while breastfeeding my daughter and the sweet smell of milk now mingled with the heady aroma of oil, talcum powder and balm; though the gown was washed often it still retained its strange smell which my dog loved. She would curl up on the dressing gown at night and if I tried to pull it away she would growl softly. As she grew old, clumps of her grey and white fur began to cling to the balding velvet.

I have worn the dressing gown for many winters now and every time I try half-heartedly to discard it my daughter protests. 'You will look like someone else if you get another dressing gown.' My husband too likes its faded pale colour, and when I bring it out to wear on the first chilly morning of winter he always says 'Winter is here'. My son, though fastidious about everything else, still loves its soft mouldy texture and when he was a child he would cling to the trailing belt with both hands and skate behind me as I walked around the house.

Though the pink colour has disappeared totally a small bright patch under the collar remains to remind me of the original brazen pink so hated by my great-uncle. The gold lace too has long vanished and the frilly collar no longer stands regally upright like it used to. Instead it flops tired and spent around my shoulders.

Every year when winter is over, I pack the dressing gown in a trunk along with other warm clothes in a layer of margosa leaves to protect them from insects. Before I place the gown amongst the bright new sweaters and shawls, I touch the torn pocket which my children had tugged while playing hide and seek behind me. I gather the fragile velvet and hold it against my face. I inhale its strange fragrance of milk, talcum powder, balm and hair oil. I smell my mother in it. I wrap the sleeves around my neck and the faded velvet is dull brown like my skin. I have to keep it for ever.

Bare Necessities
Joanna Traynor

As a child I wore frocks of gingham, rosebuds, stripes and sometimes just plain ones. All the girls wore frocks, white socks and T-bar shoes that we scuffed on day one. We weren't involved with those dresses. They didn't define us in any way. We wore them and ripped them climbing trees, fighting, jumping through hedges. They were long enough to cover our knickers and wide enough for giant sized strides over ditches, railway lines, graves of young kids we'd never know. We didn't care about fashion or dress sense. But, of course, the moment must come, does come and did come for me, when I was about nine. When I did care.

We lived up North in a town grey with industrial smoke and pessimism. No horizons. The nearest beach for a holiday was Rhyl and, every year, everyone we knew went there. Same week, same caravan park. Mum and Dad wanting more adventure, decided to test out our rusty old Anglia and so took it and us to Devon for a camping holiday. I should say right now, that my mum and dad weren't my real mum and dad. And my brother (who I won't even dignify with a name) was not my real brother.

On our very first morning we woke up to sun, just visible through the thin canvas of our tent. Sun meant we'd be off to the beach. After plastic bowls of soggy cornflakes, a luxury not afforded at home, we set off. We took with us everything we'd need for the whole day. Like my frocks, it was all homemade.

When we got to the beach, Dad dished out some dosh for the deck chairs and a windbreak. Mum had all the bags with the clobber in – sarnies, cossies, cold drinks and flasks of tea. The sea was flat, the sand brown and there were rows and rows of people just like us, doing what we were about to do – stripping off. Mum gave my brother a towel and a pair of trunks. And then, and this is it... then she held up a pair of shorts. For me. Big white shorts that had once belonged to him. She wanted me to wear my brother's cast-off shorts.

'Couldn't get you a cossie so you'll 'ave to wear these,' she said. They were HUGE. Like big white floppy underpants. They had a brass button and a zip. Flies. His flies. I looked around the beach. All the girls were wearing those navy blue suits with a pleated white skirt; little bathing frocks. Some girls even had bikinis on. How could I play at being best swimmer, best at cricket, best stone skimmer, best wave rider, best anything... wearing those shorts? If my brother hadn't been there, I might have pretended to be a boy. But he *was* there. And he was laughing at me.

Mum dangled the shorts in the air, tormenting me. He inched his trunks on, under his towel, sniggered and then pushed me towards her. Then he ran off, arms in the air, straight to the sea, to join all the other kids splashing each other, laughing in the sun. They were like a net of thin white stick insects, waiting to snare me. I was fat. I was black. I was without a bathing costume. So I had no choice. I refused to wear those shorts.

'C'mon, get 'em on,' she said. 'Stop standing there in the way of the sun and get these shorts on.'

Being one of those mothers who didn't ask, care, discuss or take no for an answer, she also didn't notice how bothered I was by all this. She took my obedience for granted. I was used to being controlled, forced, powerless. In those days, most children were. Opinions were a luxury we couldn't afford but what about dignity? That, at nine years old, was something I'd fight for.

The beach was a wildlife panorama of gaggling, white-skinned, pimpled human geese, squawking at their young, preening, oiling themselves. I looked upon the scene and shuddered. Their contentedness. The children I feared were already on to me. Eyeing me. Like young chicks, testing the waters outside the nest, they came towards me for a peek and then darted back.

'I don't wanna wear them,' I said, as loud as I could.

'What did you say?'

I was that Oliver boy asking for more food.

'I can't wear *them*,' I said, pointing at them.

'What did you say?' She was shouting now. Behind her I could see a family, mum and dad and two daughters, staring straight at us, at me. 'What did you say?'

She threw down the shorts to deal with the more immediate matter of my disobedience, open disobedience. For her, clothes were like food. Bare necessities that weren't up for negotiation. Yet here I was, complaining. For this poor mother of mine, my disobedience was the thin end of a wedge she couldn't afford. For me, that wedge wasn't so thin. To give in to her would be setting a course I didn't want to go on, look forward to, live out. How I wished I was only five years old and didn't care. We were both right. We were both wrong. For the first time ever, I felt brave enough to scream at her.

'I'm not wearing them. You only care about him. You can't make me wear them.' Bringing my brother into the argument wasn't such a good move. He was such a good boy. Where was he? Over there, all happy and out of her hair. Where was I? Sobbing in the sand, making a spectacle of the family. I felt myself losing ground.

'Listen young lady...' She grabbed my arms and slapped me. She slapped me hard and I gagged on the pain and then, with all the insides of me wanting to get out, I yarled out so long and loud, I couldn't breathe properly. I coughed and spluttered. My chest went in and out, in and out, really fast. My body was out of control. It was panicking. I was losing. Something was being taken away from me, and I cried it off, like a grieving.

'I'm not wearing them.'

I suppose to her, those cries were disobedience, insolence, the cries of a child digging her heels in. I tried to scream out one loud and long last time but out of my mouth came nothing, just an aching. As I relaxed into the inevitable, I gave it one last go.

'I'm not wearing them,' a dying sob by then.

I yanked myself away from her. I heard her growl. She got up and slapped me again, hard. She pulled me towards her with a final furious force. A nightmare beyond my wildest, because now I didn't even have a towel or the cover of the windbreak. I was to be laid bare. She was going to put me in those shorts by hook or by... by forcing me to stand there still, by forcing me to raise my arms, by pulling my frock over my head without undoing the button at the back, by pulling down my pants, so that I stood, naked, in clear view of everyone, so that I stood and no longer fought. So that I stood passive and submissive to her will, lifting my leg and holding on to her shoulder, shivering with cold and trauma – until at last, I placed my legs inside the shorts.

'Now go and play.'

I walked away from my family towards the sea with every child this side of France staring at me. I was hot, shocked, gone out of myself. I got to the water and let the cool waves flow over my feet. I stood, looking down, not daring to look around me. I stood there for quite some time. My brother, after a while, came and took a photograph of me. Me in my shorts. His shorts. He wanted to capture the moment. He did.

My Father's Greatcoat

Stevie Davies

The pacifist-to-be daughter of Mars, I bivouacked beneath his
Airforce coat. Through a succession of brown-linoed houses,
innocent of central heating, I was a spartan only child who
pattered barefoot through alien space, warming the chill floors
with my footsteps. In camp after camp from Egypt to
Germany, I fleetingly colonised territory from which I was
forever destined to be 'posted'. When the time came to move
on, I wept bitter tears in the wardrobe, up the skirts of the
greatcoat.

There were officers and there were 'men'. We were 'men'.
'Men' apparently needed neither carpets, nor more than the
most rudimentary heaters and curtains. Planes roared off over
the rooftops, night after night, where my mother and I huddled
down, in the brick equivalents of tents, marooned everywhere,
nowhere, in squadrons of nomads among the vast and obscure
hinterland of the settled. We were essential, it was said, to the
Cold War. My father was our sanctuary and his greatcoat a tent
within the tent. Airforce issue, heavy, stiff and fibrous, it could
be fought off its coat hanger and rigged on the floor, punched
up into a cone, its skirts flaring. In the darkness of this
clandestine interior, a ghost of smoke from his cigarettes
pervaded a giggly, commandeered privacy. A fighting man's
wear was subverted into a bulky Wendy house.

How did he come to be so maternal, my Forces father? For
when I look back, he is seen stooping to tender offices:

clearing up my sick, my tears, hunkering companionably in the wardrobe with me when I could not be coaxed from my tabernacle of grief. In a life of inchoate complexities (tagging along in the wake of a dying empire), the ambivalence of the blue-black greatcoat recalls both bruise and healing. The perilous absence of roots; the warmth of a portable refuge.

A belt with a bronze buckle, whose spike stabbed your fiddling fingers; buttons with embossed eagles spreading their wings (much spit and polish went in to maintaining the eagles' pride of flight). Epaulettes and a great collar.

There was pathological concern in our household about keeping warm. When the siren went, the men had to turn out in the cold. Buttoning the greatcoat with caggy fingers, forage cap at an angle, my father made ready to hare off into the night. My mother's anxious hands turned up the collar.

'Keep warm.'

'I will. Go back to sleep, my beauty.' He kissed her. 'And you, ruffian.'

Kneeling on a stool at the window, I observed our neighbouring menfolk clodhop into the smeary lamplight, their breath clouding the air: they had the hunted look of a fleeing army. What they were meant to be doing, I hadn't a clue. Drill for when the Russians came, I idly supposed. Even then, Airforce life seemed like play-acting. It involved parading, saluting and barking like dogs or being barked at.

Where were we? East Anglia, Mönchen Gladbach, Kinloss? It was all the same to us. When my father came in, creakily tiptoeing over the lino to where I was tucked up in a chrysalis of blankets (for I must be kept warm at all costs in the general hypothermia), I'd feel a heavy quilt descend. Half-surfacing, I'd moan, 'I'm warm enough, I don't need it.'

'You might not now. But there's a frost out there.'

He'd come indoors from that burning frost; from the sheen of moonlight on the chill metal of aircraft that taxied from floodlit innards of hangars. A smell of oil drifted; oil and fags.

He padded away. All night long I'd be subliminally aware of the greatcoat's dictatorial weight, the scratch of fibre on my chin. Sometimes I'd wrestle it off; at others curl gratefully in the rubber-smelling, frowsty depths with my hot-water bottle, having shaped the stiff material into a whale's hump.

In the morning, I'd sit up in bed to finger the embossed buttons meditatively. In pantomimic bliss I might lug and hunch it on to my own shoulders and, dressed to kill, goose-step around my room, with one forefinger under my nose to represent a Hitler moustache, performing berserk Nazi salutes in the mirror. My father would be aghast at this political confusion: 'Do you know what your life would have been like if they'd won?'

I didn't. But they hadn't. We had the Cold War now. Shrugging, I surrendered the coat.

Every couple of years off he went in battle-dress, a kitbag on his shoulder, greatcoat on his back, jaunty and sad at the same time. We would follow when he'd found a billet.

'Don't cry until he's gone,' my Trojan mother pleaded.

I'd gaze out through a screen of tears, through net curtains, wondering whether he was on this steeply banking plane or that.

Months later we would follow, having inventoried the contents of the quarters, with that round-the-world trunk which now, at rest, holds my grown-up son's childhood toys in his attic room. It is still marked, '522089, Flight-Sergeant Davies, H.J.' We live near Manchester Airport. Waking in the night to the muffled snarl of planes through triple-glazing, I occasionally feel the ghost of that hampering, warm weight of greatcoat and imagine that, though he's long flown, we've at last caught up. After all, we always did.

Talking Through Her Hat
Catherine Dunne

She sits, still and sepia-coloured, her arms outstretched towards the camera. Both hands rest on the ornate bone handle of an umbrella. The left hand is uppermost, and, if I look closely, I can see both her narrow gold wedding band, and the guard-ring that sits close to it. Her gaze is stern, her chin slightly tilted, her back ramrod straight. I wonder how long my grandmother had to hold that pose before the photographer finally released her. I imagine that corseted body taking a sigh of relief, heart fluttering, hand held up to the ample, silk-clad bosom.

But the strongest magnet which draws me into her photograph is the hat. It is the hat which fascinates. Although I know little about late nineteenth-century fashion, except what Hollywood and old family photographs choose to tell me, I know that *this* is the hat of a lady. Silently, it demands my attention. It proclaims Gan's social status, and the professional standing of her husband, my grandfather, more clearly than any words. It is a vast confection, full of shaded fruits and tall, undulating feathers, with at least one tiny bird nestling in the gauzy recesses of yards and yards of tulle. No wonder she has to sit still.

This young bride of late nineteenth-century Belfast, married to a man at least twenty years her senior, tells me with her elegant choice of dress and accessories that she is indeed a woman of substance. The size of the matinée hat, the complexity of its ornamentation, the sheer tasteful impracticality of its design, all proclaim the economic status of her newly acquired husband, and the importance of her role as a lady of leisure, a decorative object. That she later chose to be more than her role is an indication of the lady's strength of character. With the successive births of each of her eight children she chose, with domestic help, to be a hands-on mother. Photographs show that as her family grew larger, Gan's hats grew smaller, and there is an increasing tone of no-nonsense about them. Progressively denuded of their flora and fauna, they are tied simply under the chin with lengths of ribbon so that the chores she loved, of digging, weeding and planting, might be undertaken with impunity. She is captured by the camera outdoors on at least one occasion, in pursuit of her maternal duties: she holds my tiny father in her arms as she strides down the long garden towards the tennis court, a sensible straw hat with a shallow crown shading her eyes from the sun. A subsequent photograph, taken later the same day, shows her keeping a watchful eye on all the hot, correctly dressed young people playing there. Teenagers hadn't yet been invented.

Her first baby, a daughter, was born in 1900; her last, my father, in 1918. It was, as we say, a 'long-tailed family'. Not too many photographs survive, but those that do show the radical social changes, accelerated by the First World War, which all of Gan's children lived through. Looking at the photo of one unidentified group of young women, dated 1925, I wonder, not for the first time, at how breasts, hips, eyes and lips all seem to change size and shape dramatically according to the fashion of the day. Gone is the heavy, restrictive formality of Gan's fabulous hat and gown; gone is the elegant, ladylike tilt of the head, eyes looking into the distance beyond the lens. Instead, in the provocative stare of this group of young women, I see intimations of things to come. They belong to the most revolutionary period in the history of fashion. They look youthful, androgynous, their tube-like figures the first shadow of the modern obsession with thinness. They are smoking. The dresses are now looser, easier; the hemline has risen to the knee for the first time ever, the waistline has dropped, the breasts are barely mentioned. But it is the hat which speaks volumes. Not yet rebellious enough to go bare headed in public, each of these young women wears a cloche. Nothing could be further from the frilly, frothy, beribboned creations of their mothers. These hats – close-fitting, still decorative with crochet or gold thread or even appliqué – have raised the volume, sharpened the tone. They speak of a rejection of that restrictive definition of femininity which had been imposed upon their mothers. They announce a new freedom in dress and attitude and herald the imminent arrival of a more independent woman, one who will soon demand her economic and sexual equality in a society forever changed by the catalyst of war.

In 'The Green Hat', a play based on the novel by Michael Arlen, we see some of the changes rocking the cradle of the postwar years. The lax morals and sexual promiscuity of the movers and shakers of Bohemian society entertained the audiences of the mid-1920s, delighting and shocking them with the bad behaviour of the upper classes. The same green hat, worn on stage by Tallulah Bankhead herself, became the heady symbol of the collapse of family values. The deep-crowned cloche is pulled low down on to the brows, emphasising eyes which no longer look beyond the lens. La Bankhead's stare is direct, challenging. The hat of the moment, fitting snugly over a simpler hairstyle, becomes the accessory of the woman who demands that her rights to freedom be taken seriously, the woman who means business.

However, for the next ten years or so, that business had to be put on hold. The fashions of the hungry thirties give eloquent expression to the split personality of that era. Serious economic difficulties characterised the early years of the decade, and the latter part saw Europe plunged yet again into another war to end all wars. David Bond, in his history of twentieth-century fashion, notes that subdued colours and changes in necklines accurately reflected the mood of the times:

> All the fashion lines, as if reflecting the slump, drooped downwards. Hats were either skull caps with draped folds at the sides and back, or modified cloches with brims that dipped down over one eye. Necklines were cut to fall into rather monastic-looking cowls, and shoulders looked very sloping…[1]

And so the thirties hat, drooping over one eye, speaks symbolically of the enforced limitation of vision of the erstwhile twenties butterfly. The flapper is forced back into black, navy or grey, her plunging hemline in keeping with the lowering of spirits all around her. Interestingly, I have no surviving family photographs of the early thirties – I imagine that the times imposed a thriftiness and frugality which did not allow for such luxuries. There was, of course, another side to the thirties, for those who could afford it. Economic distinctions have always been with us, but the thirties seemed to forge an even greater dichotomy between the haves and the have-nots. By the middle of the decade, things, including the brims of hats, were looking up for the haves. The have-nots, on the other hand, could always fantasise about the glamour of the golden age of Hollywood, a glamour totally absent from their own lives. Right through the thirties, forties, and into the fifties, the movies provided an escapist world of outrageous dressing, luxurious living, and the daftest of all possible hats:

> Hats that looked like pancakes, and hats that looked like dunce caps. Hats with cabbage roses on top, feathers on

the side, drapes under the chin, and veils across the foreheads, with brims that turned up and brims that turned down. Hats bigger than a bread box and hats smaller than a pillbox. Hats perched on the side of the head like rockets about to go off. Insane, calamitous, and even potentially dangerous hats ... Movie stars deserve all our respect for having to put such things on their heads and then deliver a line like: 'Will my husband live, doctor?'[2] [Not if he sees you in that hat!]

It seems that the grimmer life was for ordinary women, the sillier and more frivolous in terms of dress Hollywood became. Perhaps movies made during the darkest years of the thirties and forties did offer a valuable fantasy-escape mechanism for all cinema goers, but I suspect that misogyny lurked somewhere below its furred and feathered surface. In order to be fashionable, women had to return to garb as restrictive as that worn by my grandmother at the turn of the century. Decoration and adornment have always been part of women's expression of their femininity – but where do tight ankle-straps, six-inch heels, skirts that impede free movement and hats with the diameter of a small table fit into such expression? At what stage does the pursuit of fashion become an enslavement, and glamour an impediment?

Photographs of my parents' wedding show the reality of postwar austerity, light-years away from the planet inhabited by Greta Garbo, Hedy Lamarr and Rita Hayworth. My mother's dress is homemade and her hat, and that of her bridesmaid, is simple, tilted a little to one side, and finished with a short veil. Shortages of material and the changing role of women in society shifted the emphasis of the hat for ever. It no longer had a speaking part, it was moved offstage, relegated to the ranks of the bit-player, or occasional special guest. The practicalities of earning a living, the possibilities of equality tasted during the war years and the accompanying demand for freedom of movement meant that the hat learned to be more modest, more accommodating. Frequently, it was replaced altogether by the snood or headscarf. Although it made a brief comeback in a starring role for Christian Dior's New Look in the late forties — where large brims, worn to complement the self-conscious opulence of postwar style, were once again fashionable — the heyday of the hat was largely over.

Today, society weddings, race meetings and the ladies who lunch emphasise the full circle that the hat has turned in the past hundred years. Once again, its function is primarily to indicate social status, to proclaim economic prominence, to highlight the wearer's decorative function. The volume may be lower, the tone may be softer, but the message is still the same.

Look at me, she says, talking through her hat: I am Somebody.

No woman I know wears a hat, now. Maybe we've found other means of expression.

Or, maybe, we just have different things to say.

Notes
1 *The Guinness Guide to 20th Century Fashion*, David Bond and Guinness Publishing Limited, 1988, p80.
2 *A Woman's View: How Hollywood Spoke to Women*, Chatto and Windus Limited, 1994, p116.

The Empire Line Dress
Andrea Stuart

We do not wear dresses; we dream them. My own recurring reverie began some time in early 1997. I had begun researching a book about the Napoleonic era and it was beginning, I suppose, to reverberate in my subconscious. I awoke in the middle of the night, breathless. I had dreamed that I was Madame Recamier, the great eighteenth-century beauty, posing white against red for the painter David. The next night I dreamed again. This time, I was the Empress Josephine, floating through a *faux* tropical garden at the Château Malmaison, waiting for Napoleon. It is this dream that comes back to me, again and again. The scenery is not constant, but the outfit remains the same. Always, it is white. Sometimes it is satin, but most often muslin, a muslin so fine that it is woven under water.

The sleeves of the dress, gently puffed at the top, grip my plump arms with the firm sweetness of an old lover. The neckline scoops scandalously low over my breasts. Fabric falls from under the bosom like the drop from a sheer cliff. I am revealed, but not entirely disarmed. My defences include a diamond necklace by the jeweller Chaumet, and a pair of satin laced ballet slippers. My only protection against nature, however, is a cashmere shawl, woven from the down of Kurghize goats, softer than silk, warmer than wool, and so supple that it can be drawn through a ring. It is designed to veil the robe gracefully, without obscuring its contours.

I am draped, not dressed. The effect of the design is voluptuous, transparent. I have eschewed glittering clothes – embroidered, embossed and re-embroidered in gold and silver on top of metallic lamé – for this idealised simplicity and order. Inspired by the writings of Rousseau I embody 'the return to nature'; I am a statue of Parian marble, my dress hanging in sculptural folds. I am a column constructed in Ancient Greece or Rome, the dress a work of architecture. Dreams of democracy are gathered in every fold; the republic swirling around me like a flag. In this dress I embody those aspirations from the past that have come again to illuminate the present.

I am Josephine, and I have survived everything to wear this dress. I was born at a crossroads in history between the old world and the new, between tradition and modernity. I witnessed the crumbling of the *ancien régime*, as well as the full sweep of the revolutionary and imperial epochs. I shared the revolutionary euphoria of Paris, my adopted city; survived a blood-soaked imprisonment in Les Carmes, and narrowly escaped the guillotine. I went on to become empress of half the civilised world. I have brushed against all the the perils of my age, great and small: slavery and pirates, hurricanes and life-threatening corsets, to arrive at this moment, just after the nineteenth century was born; to wear this dress and its promise of freedom.

I am criticised, I know. A dress like this always has its consequences. They say that the cut is so low and the fabric so thin, that the viewer can't help but notice the shape of the body rather than the classical effect. One of the Parisian papers declared that 'some thoughtless females indulge in the licence of freedom rather too far, and shew their persons in a manner offensive to modesty.' Another critic declared that 'the man of delicacy' could not help but be put off by this unwarranted display of 'unwrapped wares'. Implying, as *The Habits of Good*

Society had already lamented, that 'the best dressers are always the worst women'.

Stories that I have damped down the dress with water to make it even more diaphanous have only worsened my reputation. But I do not feel wicked in this dress. Instead I feel childlike, innocent, pure. It takes me back to my Martinique childhood, where frangipani-scented air breathed heat through my thin chemise. Strange, how others do not see this child hiding behind the practised deceit of my artifice. Always, it seems, it is men who are permitted to hold on to the passions and playthings of youth, whereas women are asked to put away childish things when they trade their identity for that of the man to whom they are promised. Women's beauty, men reason, is designed to entrap them. They have no knowledge of our hidden world of play; they do not understand our delight as we plunder the dressing-up box and paint pictures with lipstick and powder.

And to be fair, they are not completely wrong. Fashion is more than just a distraction, it has always been my greatest weapon. As a Creole outsider trying to find a place in the capital of 'fashion and folly', it was the only way I knew to re-create myself as a true *Parisienne*. I have used it to project the persona with which I wish to be identified. I have always had an uncanny desire to try on, to experiment, to reinvent myself into the characters that suggest themselves through the clothes that surround me. As a fashionable woman I realise that I am a performer, one who both flaunts and constructs my femininity.

Of course my critics do not understand that the dress tells lies. I am not naked underneath; not at all. Indeed it takes inordinate cunning to create such a 'natural' effect. I conspire for hours to produce the illusion of nudity. First I layer on one of those new corsets, a 'divorce' which separates the breasts, pressing them in a fleshy shelf. Then smooth on a pair of 'gauze inexpressibles', knitted silk tights. Over both I slip 'invisible petticoats' woven in the stocking loom, like straight waistcoats drawn down over the legs, so that I can take only short mincing steps. Only then is the precious robe lowered onto me and I am safe. As every woman knows, it is the illusion of natural femininity that takes the most elaborate and painstaking construction. Do we control this process, or does it control us? Is it a path to power, or a futile frittering of our artistry and our energies?

In an Empire line dress I am appropriately attired to wander through the gardens of history. And of memory. I discover that my dresses are always significant in my dreams. They are as evocative to me as my sense of smell. Empress Josephine, I discover, relied on two things – her muslin and her own unique blend of musk – to create the right atmosphere for her seductions. The cloth matched the scent billowing around her – evanescent, aphrodisiac, engulfing the senses of her love object. She knew, as I know, that dresses are powerful. They activate our imagination; they pique our desire. Each choice – of material, colour, cut and texture – tells its own story. I am not the only woman to realise that clothes are tightly woven into the memories of my own life, and into my understanding – or my fantasies – about the lives of others.

Purple Crimplene
Sherry Ashworth

It was 1967, the summer of love, except no love was coming my way. All the other girls in my class had boyfriends, or seemed to have. Their boyfriends all had hunky, masculine-sounding names like Steve and Dave and Rick and Trev. But then it wasn't surprising. The girls in my class knew the rules; they were streetwise, went to the right clubs, wore miniskirts and had eyes like pandas.

I was not like this. I dressed like a superannuated child in check trousers and cardies. The scholarship girl in a class of the daughters of the affluent, I was always a bit of a Cinderella. I was a little immature, too, and knew it was time to get my act together. All the more so because Liz was having a party with real boys. Here was my long awaited opportunity.

I begged my mother for a new dress, and she said in the time-honoured fashion that she would see. Meanwhile, I fantasised. The dress would *have* to be purple – purple was the only colour. The Beach Boys sang feelingly about girls who wore it, and clearly such girls were fashionable, mysterious, infinitely desirable, spiritual and sexy. The dress also had to be reasonably short. Not too short, because of my podgy knees, but a bit short because, after all, it was 1967. For her part my mother insisted that the dress had to be affordable.

Thus it was that we settled for purple crimplene. I thought crimplene sounded very mod and fab, and the colour was just right – dark, vibrant, indisputably purple. Everyone would see immediately that I was the very acme of fashion. In the changing rooms at the dress shop I thought I looked very grown-up, and the fact my mother was pulling a face made me even more determined.

For those of you born after the sixties, I should explain that crimplene was a synthetic, clingy, stretchy material. This particular dress was ribbed crimplene. It was short-sleeved, and just above the knee. It would be perfect for Liz's party; my coming-out party.

Liz was one of my best friends, and she lived in a splendidly appointed house near Bishop's Avenue in Hampstead. I'd been there before and marvelled at the number of bedrooms and the fact that Liz had her own playroom. On this auspicious occasion the playroom had been converted to a party room; plates of crisps and other refreshments had been laid out, some girls I knew were milling about – and yes, there were boys!

Real, live boys – all rather good-looking, all with the self-assurance of those born into wealth. I gawped. Then I had the uncomfortable sensation of feeling out of my depth. I noticed even Liz wasn't talking to these boys – no one was – they were just the ultimate decorative touch. I stood and watched these beautiful people disport themselves.

Looking around me, I suddenly caught a glimpse of a plump girl in a purple crimplene dress, a ribbed purple crimplene dress. Her rounded stomach protruded a little way, and above it was a roll of flesh, which I recognised as that phenomenon referred to in magazines as a midriff bulge. I also recognised that girl – that girl in the mirror – was me.

Quick as a flash, I breathed in and pulled in my stomach. I looked down. Still no good. There, buddha-like, was a proud, purple crimplene stomach atop two purple crimplene swelling thighs. Luckily I had my handbag with me and immediately adjusted it so it hung in front of my stomach, obscuring the bulge from view. The relief was short-lived. Just above my cleavage I noticed two more purple crimplene bulges. I'd told my mother over and over again that I needed another bra. Gingerly I lifted my handbag so it hid my bust, but then decided this stance made me look nervously virginal. I lowered it again. I had to face the fact – I was a walking purple monstrosity. Slowly I retreated to a corner of the room where I couldn't see my reflection, and the walls would give me some cover. Self-consciousness swept over me and I looked down, to see roll after roll of ribbed purple crimplene, the material clinging faithfully to each undulation of flesh.

What on earth had possessed me to buy the dress in the first place? Why hadn't I stood sideways in the mirror to check my bulges? Why hadn't my mother stopped me getting the thing? I felt I looked stupid, and I knew I'd been stupid; I'd tried to make myself something I wasn't, but I'd ended up making myself look exactly what I was, ie fat.

The boys ignored the purple patch in the corner. I put it down to my grotesqueness; I know now that boys rarely approach a girl whose face is a mask of terror and self-consciousness. Other girls flirted with these boys; I gradually sidled along the wall, slipped out of the playroom, and wandered along the grand corridor hellbent on escaping. I noticed Liz's mum in the living room, and she saw me too.

She beckoned me in. She was sitting in an armchair by a standard lamp, and it was lovely to see a familiar face. I asked if I could talk to her, I sat down, and intuitively she realised what was wrong. Like my own mother, she dredged up the old clichés about there being a time for boyfriends, and Liz and I were still very young, and one day it would happen, and at my age she hadn't started thinking about boys. While I listened I helped myself to some peanuts in a bowl on the table. I might as well eat. It was going to be the only physical comfort I'd get that evening, and since my bulges could hardly be any bigger or more conspicuous, a few peanuts, even a whole bowl of peanuts, wasn't going to make much difference.

I never wore my purple crimplene dress again. I stashed it at the back of my wardrobe, and its ignominious end was as a wrap for my sister's record collection when an opportunist burglar removed the records from our Hackney flat in the seventies. The discarded dress lay in a heap on the bottom of the floor of the lift.

I still remember vividly the night I wore it, and realise it gave me a kind of anti-epiphany. My flesh had manifested itself for the first time in my sight, and I realised from that moment that high fashion was not for the likes of me. I was sad to give up the dream of being a Twiggy-Cathy McGowan-Sandie Shaw sort of female, and learned that I was the one who was always destined to be in the kitchen at parties.

But by the seventies I'd learned that that was no bad thing. The kitchen was where the food was, and also where young men used to hang out, those who felt too inadequate or shy or self-conscious to compete on equal terms with butch, arrogant womanisers. These kitchen refugees were always the nicest men, the easiest to talk to, and grateful for my company. I was rarely without a boyfriend, and also never without a baggy cheesecloth shirt to hide my bulges, in black, perhaps, or white, but never, ever purple.

Finty MacKenzie's Bras
Freya North

When Finty MacKenzie was twelve, she had her first taste of humiliation. Indeed, she was force-fed an enormous portion of it. She almost choked on it, gagging on the sauce of embarrassment and the garnish of defeat that accompanied it. The decidedly insalubrious place-setting of a department store changing room had served to exacerbate matters. The curtain was far too flimsy to masquerade as a privacy screen, and far too beige and synthetic to be of any comfort whatsoever. Furthermore, every time Finty's grandmother, or the elderly sales assistant, poked their heads through the hideous drapes (which they did with alarming regularity), they appeared disconcertingly disembodied.

'How's that one, darling?'

'Better fit, young lady?'

They had to ask, because Finty certainly wasn't going to display the results. So they had to rely entirely on the brace of her small back, the angle of her bowed head and the tone of her thin voice, invariably forcing out the admission: 'Bit too big – again – I think.'

Finty MacKenzie was being fitted for her first bra.

After an hour and a half, seventeen different models, and the futile suggestions of padding with cotton-wool balls, or sewing in clumps of soft foam purchasable by the metre from Haberdashery on Second, it was concluded that there was no bra that fitted Finty. No bra small enough. None in existence for the non-existent. Come back again, dear. Next year, perhaps. When you've grown a bit, when you're a bigger girl, a young lady. When you have a breast for a bra.

'Bee stings!' her grandmother had announced, quite kindly, with a kiss to Finty's forehead and a consolatory knickerbocker glory from the Café on Fourth, 'bee sting bosoms were all the rage in the twenties. And Women's Lib,' she continued triumphantly, 'bras aren't to be worn nowadays, but burned instead!'

Was Finty meant to be grateful? Finding it impossible to respond, she ensured that her mouth was continually full of ice-cream while her grandmother discoursed on the history of feminism, arriving back at the present day and what she was going to watch on the television that night.

It wasn't that Finty minded the fact that her breasts resembled bee stings. She didn't have a problem with that. Frequently she inspected them, quite dispassionately, in the mirror in her bedroom, in the reflection of the navy blue tiles in the bathroom, and deemed their aesthetic merits to be rather high, actually. No, what Finty minded was that, apparently, bee stings did not warrant bras. Bras, it seemed, to her utter consternation, were merely contraptions of a specific function. Containers. That they could also be dreamy garments of adornment, regardless of cup size or the wearer's age, seemed to have gone unnoticed by manufacturer, shop assistant and grandmother alike.

'You don't *need* a bra, dear,' the lady from Lingerie had declared at the start, after the swiftest of glances at the be-vested Finty.

'But I'd rather like one,' Finty had held out assertively, having heard somewhere that the customer is always right.

'How about a nice new nightie?' her grandmother had suggested diplomatically, gesturing towards the tempting rails of winceyette in a stunning spectrum of pastel shades.

'Well,' Finty had said, placing her hands on her hips and staring at the hideous curtains, 'couldn't I just *try* some?'

Ten years on, Finty MacKenzie now owns a magnificent, definitive collection of bras and possesses a fine bust to go in them.

She had returned to the department store with her grandmother a year later and they had come away jubilant with a size 28AAA, white *broderie anglaise*, gorgeous first bra. Grandmother needed to sew only the slightest of darts in each cup, and a press stud along the back strap, to ensure a perfect fit. For five years, Finty grew an average inch and a half in bra size annually and trips to the department store became a yearly institution. Now she's twenty-three and a 36B, happy as punch with her bunch. More than a handful's a waste.

Finty judges many things in life by her bras. When purchasing new clothes, great consideration is given to which bra the garments will enhance. She has never bought a bra to go with an outfit, always vice versa. Down to shoes, even. She has a beautiful, french lace balconette bra, as rich in colour and texture as the finest of rum truffles. Inevitably, when she saw the brown suede court shoes not in the sale in Russell and Bromley, she knew the pairing would be perfect so she bought them with funds intended for a holiday in Lanzarote.

And men. Men too. Finty prides herself on knowing intrinsically which bra will suit which boyfriend. Her first relationship, with Richard, when they were both sixteen, necessitated a sporty crop top to expedite the athletic fumblings of youth. Since then she has always chosen men to complement her bras. She has never bought a bra to solicit a man, or on account of a man; she would not compromise her self-respect so.

William was nice. They were at college together and he seemed to suit the Marks & Spencer underwired cotton of those frugal days. Then there was Max, the marketing manager at her first job. He had been just right for the extravagance of the Rigby and Peller satin ensemble she had treated herself to, a trophy to mark her appointment as junior production assistant. Fabio, in Capri, had gone wonderfully with the minuscule bikini from the Next Directory – and the bikini looked very good next to his even more microscopic posing pouch. There was the one night stand in the bra she wore only once. And the relationship she felt trapped in – finally extricating herself only when realising with horror that she had taken to wearing an old bra, once white, now chewing-gum grey and more threadbare by the day.

And now Matt. Tonight. The all important, eagerly anticipated third date when all manner of revelations, emotional and physical, were bound to transpire. Hopefully.

'So, who is it to be?' Finty asks the contents of the drawer kept exclusively for her bras and skilfully compartmented by a master carpenter to Finty's precise specifications. The velvet and mesh half cup catches her eye but Finty decides it clashes with Matt's coolness and reserve which she finds so attractive, so disconcerting, so magnetic. How about the ivory silk – no, not that one, the one over there, the one with the tiny, cleavage-kissing rosebud?

'Too pure, and therefore,' Finty sighs, 'too deceptive. Can't lie. I like him, you see. Don't want to put him off.'

How about the basque?

'Don't think so. No.'

Piped satin?

'Which? The black one?'

Or the peach.

'No.'

Or the navy.

'Nope.'

Freya North

Silk satin muslin cotton lace devoré thermal. Stretch sheer opaque shiny soft matt padded plain. Pull-on rip-off. Under-wired half cup front fastening low back halter necked seamless strapless wonder bra. Wonderful bras. Cross your heart.

'It must be *right*,' says Finty, slightly exasperated, placing her hands either side of the drawer. 'I really rather like him,' she explains to her bras, 'so it's got to be *me*.'

Finty has no idea that, a few miles away, Matt is tearing out his hair as to which boxers he should wear. He has a vast collection, accumulated from the day he cashed his grant cheque and spent a notable percentage on five, pure silk, polka-dotted, Simpson of Piccadilly finest.

'Lecture halls,' he had said to himself as much as to the sales assistant, 'are notoriously uncomfortable.'

Currently, Matt has whittled his choice down to any one of fourteen pairs. He has fanned them out on his bed and is pacing his room, arms crossed and finger crooked over his lip in deliberation.

'Who wants to meet Finty?' he asks out loud. They all do, it appears. 'Don't make me toss for it,' Matt warns but knows that this is the only solution. Naked from the waist down, he goes in search of small change.

Matt and Finty had a wonderful evening, prophetic of what they both hope will develop into a good relationship. They went back to her place. Finty hardly noticed Matt's navy and dark gold stripy Ralph Lauren boxers. Her eyes, her interest and her criteria were elsewhere.

And you, Finty? Which did you finally choose? What greeted Matt's gaze when you slithered out of your little black dress?

'I wanted to be myself, remember. And I felt surprisingly comfortable. Actually, I did not wear a bra at all.'

Socks

Kate Mosse

I am lying on my bed at the age of thirteen, arms behind my head, experiencing adult nerves in my child's stomach. Waiting. The light is fading outside, turning the greens and browns and whites of my Habitat room to black. The smell of dusk is so strong that I think I could reach out and touch it, everything so peaceful and muffled and slow. I register the sounds of the kitchen table being laid for dinner, the familiar clatter of knives and forks and spoons. I'm half-aware of an escalating fight between my sisters over whose turn it is to have the stool. Realise it must be just before six o'clock. It's all too distant to bother me.

I sit up. Cross my legs. Tap my fingers on my knees. This time tomorrow it will be over. My first rehearsal for the West Sussex Youth Orchestra, a group that meets at the end of each holiday to put together a concert from scratch. I've been warned by my terrifying violin teacher that I'll be one of the youngest and that nobody I know got in with me at the last round of auditions. There are a few fifth and sixth formers from my school in it already, sure. But they don't count. They won't have a clue who I am.

I'm worried about humiliating myself. Of not knowing what to do or where to go. And as I sit on the bed in the half light, I can imagine only bad snapshots – the music too hard, the conductor too fast, standing alone in the breaks with no one to talk to.

Beyond all this, although I don't understand it yet, I'm aware of another emotion. A clean and definite feeling. What I want most is for my first time in the orchestra to be significant to other people. Not just me. I want to be noticed. And up here in the privacy of my bedroom, away from the tittle-tattling tongues of friends, I can ignore the voice in my head that tells me not to show off and not to draw attention to myself and not to push myself forward. Girls don't. Girls shouldn't.

The joke is this is supposed to be about music, but there's a one in a million chance of me making an impact as a player. I'm no child prodigy. There'll be plenty like me, talented and enthusiastic players, good enough to take their place in the orchestra but not good enough to lead it. In any case, a quality string section thinks and plays like a single violinist. All bows moving in the same direction, a shared dynamic, a common tempo. The best section players fit in. There is no room for character, for individuality. The whole point is not to stand out.

But clothes. There's my chance. I'm socially immature for my thirteen years, but I do understand it's possible to impress through appearance. Some have high cheekbones, straight black hair, extra inches. Most of us don't. But anybody can make themselves interesting if they dress right. I see how the older girls at school define themselves through the bits and pieces they add to their uniforms; the length of their skirt or the height of their heels or the combs in their hair.

I have no analysis of this. It will be years before feminism gives me a language and a context within which to think and make decisions. I have no comprehension of the politics of fashion, of the complicated network of motive, negotiation and pressure. Unconsciously, though, I do understand how clothes are used to distract from things that matter. How we focus on what we can – control our personal appearance – to distract ourselves from events we cannot. The challenge of an exam, an interview, a competition or a date. We concentrate on external appearance to help mark the minutes, hours, between the anticipated then and a never-ending now. Displacement activity. As an adult, I will use these words. Not yet.

I've spent pretty much the whole afternoon eating crisps and working out what to wear tomorrow. Trying stuff, rejecting skirts and trousers and tops. Figuring out the person I want to be. Everything out of my cupboard and tossed on the floor, until I'm happy. A pair of faded jeans, a white smocked shirt, a sweatshirt with a treble-clef printed on it and, most important of all, my multi-coloured, striped knee-length socks with individual toes I got last Christmas. They fulfil every requirement – they're unusual, they're envied and they make me feel special. I wear them anywhere that matters and never lend them to anybody. The only problem is that it's too cold and wet to wear sandals. And without sandals, no one in the orchestra will realise how exceptional these socks are. I've worked out the only thing to do is to casually ease off my shoes when I'm actually playing, without making too big a deal about it. The players around me will either notice the individual toes or they won't. Up to them.

I cast my eye over to the chair in the corner of the room where the outfit is precisely laid out, neat and ready for the morning. It's too dark to see clearly, but I'm confident I've struck the right note. All I can do now is wait.

I'm up and dressed before six, listening to David Essex singing 'How Can I Be Sure?' with the volume turned down. By seven, I've drunk too much tea and eaten too much toast. At ten to nine, my father is dropping me at the gate of the school where we'll rehearse for the next four days. Wednesday to Saturday. He wishes me luck as he kisses me goodbye.

I walk up the tarmac drive towards the main school building. The pavements are still slippery from the early morning mist, the air chill in my nose and back of my throat.

I feel the reassuring weight of my violin case in my hand and the scratch of the wool between my toes and on the backs of my knees. I see other people ahead of me on the path, clutching instruments of all shapes and sizes.

Following the sound of voices, I walk across the lobby to the double doors and creep in at the back. I'm in a large hall, like any other school hall in any other comprehensive school. The main stage is straight ahead, the regulation seventies-style curtains run along the back wall and the monkey bars and ropes and gym equipment fill the remaining two sides floor to the ceiling. In a hall just like this, I sit through Assembly every day, I queue up for lunch, I do drama lessons in bare feet and a leotard.

In this environment, I should feel at home. Except I don't. I feel the opposite. The atmosphere is entirely alien. Threatening, even. It's not just that everyone is in their own clothes rather than school uniform, although that is part of it. It seems as if all the girls are wearing long, Indian wrap-round skirts and beads and clogs. They're not, of course. It's just the few that set the tone for the many. All the boys have long hair and beards and take up lots of space. A few of the older ones are even standing outside on the path smoking roll-ups. There's a shadow of the adult world in here that makes me feel uncomfortable.

Did I really think people would pay attention to me? That the right clothes would get me accepted? Make me an insider? I think I did. That I really did. But I don't need to look round to know I've got it wrong. My embossed sweatshirt and cute socks expose me. I'm a kid, not one of them. I'm too young. Look too childish.

I quickly put my violin case down on the floor and flip open the catch. Unwrap my fiddle from its cloth, tighten my bow, hunt for the hard, black rock of resin in the pocket at the front. Trying to look like an old hand as embarrassment burns through me and my throat seizes up. I feel like I'm going to suffocate.

Of course no one says anything. Why would they? No one notices my confidence bleeding away. I sit on my chair – the back row of the second violins – relieved that no one is talking to me. At lunch, I rummage around in my music case, pretending I've more important things to do than make friends. Six hours later, I leave in silence and snap at my parents and refuse to answer their questions when I get home.

I'd like to lie and say I learned something. About how if you depend on others to make you feel good about yourself, you'll end up disappointed. About how the need for approval and endorsement holds you back rather than empowers you. About how we need to be satisfied with ourselves above all else. Clothes, make-up, ideas, creativity, politics; the importance of self-motivation is the same.

But at the time, all I knew was that reality had not lived up to expectation. I blamed myself for spoiling things and clung to the belief that if only I'd chosen the right clothes, then everything would've been different. All my fault. Better luck next time.

And the socks themselves? Those two strips of wool unequal to the burden set upon them? The truth is, I just can't remember. I'd like to think I defiantly wore them to every other rehearsal, as a symbol of something or other. But I suspect I stuffed them down the back of a drawer. They were painful reminders of how I'd failed, so I abandoned them as a punishment.

But now, over twenty years later, I can still picture the pattern of the colours shimmering one into the other. How the stripes melted from pink to purple to blue to green to yellow to orange to black then started over. How they pricked against my skin, how I'd pull them high up to the knee and fold them over to stop them falling down when I was running.

And I can still remember, even now, how proud they once made me feel.

My Old Green Jacket
Caeia March

I wore it for the first time to embrace the base at Greenham. Misty and cold, the weather had been causing some anxiety for weeks as London dwellers prepared for the trip. So I found myself in a camping shop in Deptford and there on the rack it was waiting for me. It had everything I needed – a waterproof outer layer in mid-green; an enormous hood that came forwards more than four inches from my face and ended in a thick inverted horseshoe shape of imitation fur; wrist straps that could be snugged tight around long thick gloves; deep pockets with overflaps like small roofs to keep the rain out; upper pockets sloping for credit cards and money; and a pocket with a zip for my car keys up high on my left sleeve.

The whole of the front of the jacket could be zipped over my chin as far as my nose so that I could look out through a furry tunnel and not an erg of warm body energy would be wasted. Inside there was a quilted polyester lining, warm as toast; and another pocket for scraps of paper and a pen.

The jacket was in the sale and I think it was about twenty pounds; the best two tenners I ever spent. From the very beginning it was soft and pliable and fitted me like a loose friendly protective layer of second skin.

We had an amazing life-changing day at Greenham, weaving woollen webs between the trees and the wire boundary fence, though I never went there to stay, and there were debates and turmoil-ridden workshops in London from those who saw saving the common as an act of betrayal of real lesbian separatism. Lesbians from the camp had a hard time being made to justify to city dykes why their struggle was as valid as urban Reclaim the Night marches. My parka saw it all. I wore it continually and it became my best coat and everyday coat for about three years.

With time the imitation fur began to look rather tatty. I looked like a medium-sized mountain bear with a terminal dose of mange. Many tubbings in my washing machine had also brought the colour down a shade or two (or four) – the newness and action glamour of my demonstration attire had definitely worn off. However, I didn't want to face the functional failure of my ageing green garment, so it came with me to a friend's house in Cornwall after Christmas 1986. My friend had announced the previous Easter that she and her husband had bought a tea shop in St Just. They had spent the early summer refurbishing it and its delightful adjacent granite cottage. The house was in the town and was very old, with two-foot thick walls and a slate roof. It was a beautiful place.

I was walking down Cot Valley when the squalls set in. Down came the mizzle – a fine form of insistent, relentless rain found only in Cornwall at its silent, hostile best. Retracing my steps along a route where unexpected early crocuses shone in the undergrowth like Solstice candles and where the invading Japanese knotweed in its winter mode resembled deep russet squirrel tails leaping for the sky, I was aware both of the raw beauty of the wild landscape and the unprepared un-weatherproofness of my erstwhile reliable coat.

Back indoors I hung my sodden jacket on a padded hanger over the ingle-nook fireplace with a resigned and grateful sigh. It had seen me through good times and bad, the break-up of a relationship, the process of falling in love again, the newly discovered passion for the land, sea and sky scapes of Cornwall, and it held a special place in my heart.

In Penzance next day we purchased its successor, but there was no way I was going to consign my old green parka to an uncertain future in somebody's outhouse by sending it to a charity shop. There were plenty to choose from had I wished to dispose of it – Penzance was hit hard by recession and charity shops were mushrooming all over the town.

But we were on holiday and I had plenty of time to think of a plan for my dried out jacket. I came up with a few ideas, put them all on hold, and lovingly packed the jacket and returned with it back to the city.

We returned in time for Clause 14 to become Clause 27/28 and a cold bleak demo in Kennington near the Imperial War Museum. My old jacket was resting at home in its box and missed seeing the police in riot gear on horseback solid in every sidestreet.

The following summer I was working one day in my partner's very pretty long garden behind her terraced house in Walthamstow. As I worked, I began to feel a bit cold, so I ran indoors and grabbed my old green jacket. But the hood was a nuisance. It was big and floppy when it wasn't zipped up. So I reached for the heavy duty kitchen scissors and in a few seconds I had a collarless gardening jacket.

I come from a long line of tailors and seamstresses on both sides, and that evening I rooted around in the bits box and found a quarter of a yard of soft velveteen left over from the curtains. An hour later my gardening jacket had a sleek, velvet and perfectly comfortable soft collar, which would make it wearable against the back of my neck at any time, even over a thin collarless T-shirt in the garden on a cool working summer's day.

However, I never managed to do as much gardening as I'd hoped during the next few years because I went down with ME. My jacket hung as a symbol of history and hope in my wardrobe, always clean and aired, ready.

Allergic to benzene in the air and to all forms of traffic vibration and fumes, I moved to Cornwall in the autumn of 1988, part time, then full time two years later.

The jacket accompanied me on that move, then from St Just to the barns where I became the tenant on Women's Land, then to Bodmin Moor where I lived for a few months in 1994, then back to the barns, then to Sennen Cove where my new partner and I rented a Hollywood style house on the cliffs for two years.

Eventually the jacket came home to White Waves. We have found a quiet haven, my jacket and I. I live here with Cheryl, safely housed at last and with a third of an acre garden, mature and established on the wild north coast. I am steadily recovering from ME though it has been a long, long haul.

We have new Women's Land here in Cornwall now. It is held in trust, not owned by any one woman, and cannot be taken away. My jacket is helping with the planting of nine hundred baby trees. From Greenham Common to a wild flower garden in a London terrace, to the native species of our tree planting project, my jacket is still green, still in the front line of conservation.

The Book Dress
Elisa Segrave

Was it a coincidence that I fetched the Book Dress out of my bedroom cupboard where it had been for over ten years, on the day that my ex-husband's girlfriend moved in with him?

We had bought the Book Dress in Paris in 1979, a year or so before we were married. When I asked my ex-husband recently about it, he reminded me that it had come from a shop in Les Halles, and that he had helped me choose it. He liked coming shopping with me. Unlike some men in their attitude to women's clothes he was patient, appreciative and interested.

The Book Dress can only be worn in spring and summer. It is of a synthetic material and hangs loose, straight to the knee. It has a black background and the whole fabric is crammed with pictures of books – white, grey, red, green and purple.

Bright colours suit me. I loved the Book Dress because it was a combination of the smart, the casual and the original. Why did I keep it in the cupboard for so long? Did I stop wearing it when I became pregnant with my son in 1983, and never put it on again? Or did I banish the poor Book Dress several years later, after I got divorced? I'm not sure.

During the early years of our courtship and subsequent marriage, my husband took the photographs and I stuck them into albums and labelled them. Now, nearly ten years later, there's an enormous backlog of loose photos on a table and it's my daughter, not me, who takes them, usually of the dog. Perhaps by now my ex-husband has accumulated a whole new set of photographs of him, his girlfriend, our children and the dog, who all visit him regularly.

Last week I went through the old albums looking for the Book Dress. It appears in Paris in April 1992, when our first baby, Lauretta, was eight months. I am holding my daughter – she still doesn't have much hair – outside the building where we had rented a flat for two weeks. The baby and I are smiling; she's in a little white dress and light blue anorak. My husband has cut off the top of my head in the photo. Round my neck I am wearing a bright red necklace of plastic popper beads which were my grandmother's. Over the Book Dress I am wearing one of my grandmother's cardigans – black with a collar edged with silver. My haircut, by a Spaniard called Pedro, is one of the most stylish I've ever had. I remember, on seeing the photo again, how quickly I lost weight after my first baby, enough to wear the Book Dress again that spring, a few months after giving birth.

Beside that photo of me in the Book Dress with my baby is another, of the three of us together, all smiling, in the Jardin des Plantes. I am crouched down, wearing red trousers and a white sheepskin jacket which a French boy had given me in 1973, when I was living in Paris as a student. My husband is sitting back on his heels and our baby is between us in a borrowed French pushchair, leaning forward and cheekily waving her rattle. Behind us are beds of yellow and red tulips.

Once someone asked me when I had been happy. I replied immediately: 'I was happy when I had my first baby and happy when I was living in Paris before that.'

I suppose that was why I had begged my husband to go there for those two weeks with our baby. I wanted to combine the two pleasures.

I had left Paris for good in September 1974 after living

there for a year. When I came back to England my father, still in his sixties, died. Subsequently I often regretted giving up my room in the Latin Quarter. Sometimes I dreamed of my attic – six floors up inside a courtyard – as a place of safety; I remember one dream in which there were pots of red geraniums on the window-sill.

We constantly readjust the past according to present desires and regrets. Memory can be both comforting and painful. Isn't the passing of time most painful of all? It is perhaps misguided of me therefore to see the Book Dress as a straightforward symbol of happiness.

My husband often said it would be a mistake for him to marry me before I had a book of my own published. I would be dissatisfied, he said. His own first book had come out soon after we met, and by the time we got married he was writing a second. I had published nothing except two articles in a newspaper. We got married anyway.

A short story I wrote appeared the month my daughter was born. That next April, in the rented flat in Paris, I remember writing a new story based on my husband's and my visit to Italy to see his brother, before we got married. (I may have worn the Book Dress in Italy.) The story depicts certain unsatisfactory elements in our relationship. So, though it is tempting to do so, it is ridiculous to look at a photograph of myself in the Book Dress now and think: 'Then I was happy.' And yet...

A few months after I met my husband he took me south to visit his friend Philip, to a village just outside Uzès. I remember how, after the dark London winter, the first time we pulled off the French motorway into a village in the mountains of the Ardèche for the night, we saw cherry blossom.

After that we would try to get away south nearly every spring, to Philip's village, Flaux. It is at Flaux that the Book Dress appears again in the album. I am standing alone on one of those straight French roads, with stumpy black vines each side. Below that is another photo of us and our baby, in Philip's kitchen, one of his wife's Persian rugs on the wall behind us. Panna had spent most of the money she had inherited from her Hungarian father, a successful surgeon in America. Soon after our visit, we heard that she was forced to work cleaning houses in her village. In the sixties, when she had lived in the Dakota Buildings in New York, she had known Burroughs and Ginsberg and had given money away to Beat poets and drug addicts.

In that snap taken at Philip and Panna's, my husband, in one of his favourite striped shirts, is leaning into the picture, and the baby, one hand to her mouth, has on a white towelling sunhat and another white dress. A bunch of purple and yellow flowers are on the table in front of us. How happy we look! I recall how once again we had stopped in the Ardèche for the night and seen cherry blossom. Does one's past life always seem so idyllic in retrospect? The broken nights, the tiredness, have all disappeared and I only remember how happy I was with my first baby.

I wore the Book Dress for only one day after I rescued it last year. I told my daughter I was going to wear it in front of her father to surprise him, but I forgot to do it. In the golden Indian summer of 1997, just after the funeral of Diana, even the light Book Dress was too hot for the streets of Notting Hill. Although the label said DRY CLEAN ONLY, I perversely decided to wash it in the machine, on a low cycle. The Book Dress shrank. I will never be able to wear it again.

I look in my diary of 1982 and read how on 27 April, Philip and Panna's cat had kittens in the Ali Baba urn in the garden, while we and the baby were sitting there. We suddenly heard squeaking from inside the urn. I read how, on the day we arrived at Flaux, Panna's son Felix, who was shy, silently let two white fantail pigeons into the dark dining room. Our baby shrieked with excitement and one bird alighted on a large vase above the oven. A few minutes later, my husband pulled a tick from the jaw of Philip's collie. Blood came out.

Now it's December. Last night we had our first snow of this winter. My ex-husband will take his girlfriend to Flaux in April. Philip is old now and dying. My baby daughter is seventeen. The Book Dress still hangs in my cupboard. I don't think I will ever throw it away.

The Denim Jacket
Alba Ambert

The coat rack features an abundance of choices. Hanging like carcasses in a butcher's shop, there are winter coats, hooded rainwear, sweaters and parkas. Markers of a time long gone, of recent preferences, of sartorial mistakes. As my eyes rest on each one, I journey an endless archipelago of people, places and events: the merino wool sweater purchased at a Como shop with its evocation of mulberry and oleander; the raw silk overcoat from a sun-washed workshop in the ochre hills of Roussillon; a boundless green cape drooping empty and forlorn; the black coat that for years shielded me from the inclement winters of New England. But before I step out the door, I reach, as always, for the faded denim jacket with the frayed collar and the seams that, with time, have puckered like chapped lips. I shrug into it easily; the fabric substantial, the cut ample and forgiving.

An early morning mist, thick as ashes, floats over the Thames as I stand at Richmond Hill Rise and finger the brass buttons embossed with tiny stars. I am back in New England. The door flies open and my daughter Yanira rushes in sporting the brand new denim jacket. I smile as she glances at herself in the mirror appraisingly. For several years she will wear the jacket constantly, with cut-off jeans and high tops, with miniskirts and high heels. In its abundance of inner and outer pockets, she will stash away lipsticks, dollar bills, a driver's license, spare change, bits of paper scribbled with phone numbers. Her anxieties and desires.

When it is warm, she hooks the jacket over a shoulder jauntily or ties the sleeves around her hips and wears it like a sensual sarong. She lies on it at the edge of the Charles River, eyes tipped to the sky. Or she rolls it up and wedges it at the nape of her neck when she stretches out on the sofa to watch TV. On the day she sets off for college in New York, suitcase packed with freshly acquired clothes that herald a new look, she leaves the jacket behind. I wear it a few times and then put it away while breaking in the elegant black coat, the merino wool sweater, the raw silk overcoat produced by the Indian weaver in Roussillon. With sobering professional responsibilities, I too have committed to a change of image, shedding the Malaysian cotton tops, the turtlenecks and faded jeans that have tempered the dryness of my years in graduate school.

Then I install an impossible distance between us. In pursuit of a dream, I move to Athens and later settle in London while Yanira takes root in New York. The ocean stretches between us, so vast our hands no longer touch; our voices silenced for long reaches of time. That's when I begin wearing her denim jacket and, while rummaging through the closets for a particle of her, I find other clothes she has tired of and given to me – dresses and T-shirts and nightgowns. I begin to wear those too and, when I do, it is her reflection I see as I stand in front of the mirror.

The contours of the Thames sharpen as the sun climbs the hill and the mist begins to draw away. Still, I shiver and pull the jacket tightly around me. Once more, I inhabit my daughter's skin. My gaze drifts to the far reaches of nostalgia and I look out at the world as she has seen it. I ache with her fear and desolation when she's nine years old and we abandon the solace of everything we have known in our native Puerto Rico and set off for Cambridge, Massachusetts, filled with all the expectations of a new beginning. From the time of my divorce when Yanira was four and I was twenty-two, we had faced the world together with equanimity. In Puerto Rico, we relished the voluptuous raiments of an island of sun and sea and palm trees rustling in the wind. We were attired in the comfort of the familiar, of the predictable. The island was our vernacular and we conversed in it with ease. Protected by the impermeable borders of the island, we were ill prepared for the uncompromising chill that the immense northern continent reserved for the outsider.

In my daughter's skin, I get off the school bus in Cambridge and cry out when the gang of schoolchildren attacks. I am knocked down with her on that hard Cambridge pavement. She shields her head with her arms as the torrent of blows falls on her. She slaps her hands to her ears when the ugly faces yell: 'Filthy spik, filthy spik,' a refrain that resounds through the thick crust of decades, never to be forgotten. I wipe my face as she wipes hers when the angry mouths spit on her.

A drop of rain slips down my cheek like a tear. I look up at the clouds, sullen and fat. Every afternoon, the gang attacks and Yanira curls into herself like a foetus. In her denim jacket, I face her fear of leaving the apartment where she seals herself from the world. Together, we become an island and with our bare hands build a frontier against the rocks hurled through our bedroom windows, the spray-scrawled message of hate on our door. We turn our backs on the neighbors who judge us harshly, not recognising who we really are, but seeing us as the vicious gang members of *West Side Story*, the drug-addled prostitutes of *Fort Apache, The Bronx*, or the cold-blooded murderers of *Serpico*. We learn to live in the silence of our own language.

The years in Cambridge, Massachusetts, harden us. An edge of mistrust informs our choices as we gather friends around us, cautiously, selecting them like precious stones. At school, Yanira befriends the atheist who won't participate in morning prayers, the pinko teacher who introduces her to Ariel Dorfman's *How to Read Donald Duck*, the Armenian girl with the cowboy boots. She surrounds herself with the familiarity of the marginal.

Always alert to false diamonds and counterfeit currencies, we glance at each other with suspicion when a man shows up out of nowhere and looks at me longingly. We wonder what he wants. How long it will be before the slur slides from his tongue and blinds us with anger. He's awfully nice, we say. But still we wonder. We take a walk through Harvard Square while I consider his strengths out loud. Yanira cries, 'But, Mami, he's white!' and plunges her hands into the jacket's ample pockets.

We let him in and our reality shifts. We learn to expect kindness and trust. And we return the bounty. He is encumbered with family and friends. But they are suprisingly like him. Our defenses loosen as we open ourselves to new possibilities. When Walter gives me his late mother's ring, Yanira and I huddle together in bed and plan for the wedding. Before the ceremony, Yanira brings out an arsenal of hairspray, powder brushes and eyeliners. She braids my hair and coils the braids around my head. Into the coil she tucks a sprig of baby's breath. She paints my face with the concentration of a lace maker. I can smell the sweetness of her breath when she says, 'Close your eyes,' or 'Turn this way.' At noon, when we brace ourselves to face the Justice of the Peace, she smooths the creases on my dress. She stands by my side to bear witness and holding my hand, she puts my other hand in Walter's. After the reception, she finds the denim jacket in the coat closet, shrugs into it and makes the long journey to New York. All that night I'll wonder whether the jacket is warm enough.

The air is crisp as I head home. When I walk in the door, a pale ray of sunlight breaks through the clouds. I remove my daughter's denim jacket and rub it against my cheek before hanging it on the coat rack. I finger the thick fabric, the soft lining. The buttoned cuffs and collar that keep the wind out. It is definitely warm enough.

The Dernier Cri
Catherine Temma Davidson

Unwilling to let three women in their thirties handle the grave responsibility of finding her daughter's wedding dress, my mother has flown from Los Angeles to San Francisco to run interception. My friend Diane is driving, my mother is in the front seat, my sister and I are in the back, and we are crossing the Bay Bridge to go to Marin where we have heard there are stores selling antique dresses.

'What are you wearing?' she asks me, and I shrug, as if to say look for yourself: shorts, a T-shirt, high tops. The day is warm. 'No, underneath – bra, slip, stockings?' I had imagined us trooping into the store in our summer gear, handling a few pieces of lace, picking something up almost as an afterthought, a joke. 'You see why you need me...' As if as an aside, my mother asks, 'And how much do you weigh these days?'

'That's it,' I finally shout at her. 'That kind of question is absolutely off-limits.' I am suddenly fourteen. My sister tells Diane to turn on the radio.

There is a picture of my mother in her wedding dress, getting married at the Overseas Press Club in Manhattan. It is the fifties; she has the perfect fifties body and a dress to fit it – tight at the waist, a scoop neck, plain silk. She looks impossibly glamorous and free. Because she married my father across religious boundaries, they had a wedding without many relatives – full of smart-talking young men and women in two-piece suits and thick-rimmed glasses, holding martinis and cigarettes. Once, I tried on her dress. The bust hung off me and the waist was too small. She was the same age as I was when I got married, but she seemed older somehow, more of a woman. She was motherless, self-generated; she smoked and drank. During one of our fights I tried to tell her this.

'My mother wasn't alive to help me get married. I *had* to do it on my own.' That shut me up.

By July I was regretting my pledge to devote a whole summer to the project of wedding preparation in Los Angeles, with my mother happy arm in happy arm. From the distance of a London winter, it had seemed like the right decision – a mother daughter thing. This one last time, I would be the perfect, sweet-tempered child I had never been. I had forgotten how many disasters we had encountered in the past on shopping expeditions; my mother always wanting to buy me the feminine, Katherine-Hepburn-about-town tailored outfits, while I was always reaching for the starving-artist-just-off-the-co-operative denim overalls. I felt guilty. I was getting married – I was leaving her. The whole summer it hung over us like a cry – the '*dernier cri*' as my mother said dramatically one night while we were trying on make-up together. If only we knew. Being married is easy if you can survive the wedding.

It was not really a wedding dress. It was a living Rorschach test: my feelings about my body, my mother's feelings about my body, my feelings about her body, her feelings about her body. When I told her I wanted to wear comfortable shoes, she told me not to be ridiculous. We compromised with half a heel, expensive but well made.

I escaped to San Francisco, the city where I had attended my first lesbian wedding, because it was a place where I thought I could buy a wedding dress in the suitable spirit of kitsch. It became clear after a few weeks that Los Angeles would never yield the dress of my dreams. My mother and I had spent hours together driving past endless mini-malls with the air conditioner blasting. In the all-inclusive wedding stores with their white leather divans, I could see that to get married was to be Queen for a Day: tiaras and sequins, seed pearls to make a Renaissance princess gasp, tight waists and full skirts. Words I had learned reading thick historical romances under the covers in my girlhood came back to me: muslin, tulle, *décolletage*. The trouble was that my reading had not stopped there; I had graduated on to other, more sceptical women writers. How does a feminist get married to a man? How do you explain your ambivalence to a mother – Greek by birth, Jewish by inclination – whose first daughter you are?

I wish I could say that I handled it well. Once, when emerging from a dressing room up to my neck in satin, a helpful attendant suggested that it was a lovely dress. 'Don't call it a dress,' I told her with tears in my eyes. 'Call it a ritual robe for my public commitment ceremony.'

For my friend with the PhD - red, *fin de siècle*, looped in silk roses, bubbly as a glass of champagne; for the struggling performance artist – severe, pale ivory, a captive going to her death; for the psychotherapist who took her husband's name – flounces and a crown; for the rebellious second-generation Pakistani – a jewel-encrusted salwar kameez, on loan from traditionalist cousins in Minneapolis; for the daughter of a union organizer, sheer pink over layers of gold satin with orange feathered head-dress to wear to her wedding in a rented Yorkshire castle. In their wedding dresses, none of my friends looked like themselves.

*

The air in Marin County is much hotter than it was in
Berkeley, where my sister lives. Diane is wearing a cotton
minidress and combat boots. My sister has on jeans and a
sleeveless top — her underarm hair shows. My mother is
dressed in navy silk and stockings; she marches into the store
first. For a moment, I want to grab Diane's hand and head for
the hills. We are so used to playing with the symbols of being
a woman — we can talk lipstick and the semiotics of lipstick.
Wedding dresses are harder to get around. We are in a no-go
area, and my mother is our troop leader. Following into the
store, we blink at the sudden loss of sunlight.

In the end, it is impossible to be ironic about a wedding dress.
Weddings are our last public ritual. You are stepping into a role
that is bigger than you are, and if you understand the history
of that role, it is bound to terrify you. Still, as they say in the
glossy magazines, when I saw the dress, I just knew. It was a
dress to be worn at a tea party on the Titanic, layers of ivory
antique lace arranged à la 1912 — romantic but with room to
move. Used to upmarket hippies, the woman behind the
counter did not blink at my black underwear and frayed bra-
straps. It was something both my mother and I could imagine
for a wedding, and fit the compromise we had reached
between her large Oscar-night hotel reception with silver and
crystal and my vision of a ceremony in a public park, with
Styrofoam cups. I was getting married in a rose-covered
Victorian house by the beach in Santa Monica, and I was
going to wear a wedding dress.

I decided to wear a veil one day a few weeks later after
having a panic attack in a parking garage. I imagined my
husband's English relatives arriving with pastel hats and
expectations. I imagined the American relatives, having flown
several thousand miles in some cases, full of anticipation. Had
I gone too far? How would anyone know that I was that

precious thing – a bride? We got the material at a fabric warehouse on Third Avenue, near the Orthodox temple. Maybe it was the men with large beaver hats walking past the window, or the stout-armed woman in orange polyester rolling out the soft, pale fabric and offering a discount. Something made me feel extravagant. I was in Hollywood after all; it was a costume, and this was a production whose credits were shared. I told my mother – make the veil as long as you like, just don't expect me to wear it over my face. In the photographs from the wedding it trails behind me, far below my waist, like the hair made of seaweed I used to place on sandcastle princesses, so I knew which lump of sand was which. There was no doubt in anyone's mind, and little doubt in my own, who was the bride, who was the star of the show.

A Red Shirt

Margaret Atwood

(For Ruth)

i.
My sister and I are sewing
a red shirt for my daughter.
She pins, I hem, we pass the scissors
back & forth across the table.

Children should not wear red,
a man once told me.
Young girls should not wear red.

In some countries it is the colour
of death; in others passion,
in others war, in others anger,
in others the sacrifice

of shed blood. A girl should be
a veil, a white shadow, bloodless
as a moon on water; not
dangerous; she should

keep silent and avoid
red shoes, red stockings, dancing.
Dancing in red shoes will kill you.

ii
But red is our colour by birth-

right, the colour of tense joy
& spilled pain that joins us

to each other. We stoop over
the table, the constant pull

of the earth's gravity furrowing
our bodies, tugging us down.

The shirt we make is stained
with our words, our stories.

The shadows the light casts
on the wall behind us multiply:

This is the procession
of old leathery mothers,

the moon's last quarter
before the blank night,

mothers like worn gloves
wrinkled to the shapes of their lives,

passing the work from hand to hand,
mother to daughter,

a long thread of red blood, not yet broken

iii

Let me tell you the story
about the Old Woman.

First: she weaves your body.
Second: she weaves your soul.

Third: she is hated & feared,
though not by those who know her.

She is the witch you burned
by daylight and crept from your home

to consult & bribe at night. The love
that tortured you you blamed on her.

She can change her form,
and like your mother she is covered with fur.

The black Madonna
studded with miniature

arms & legs, like tin stars,
to whom they offer agony

and red candles when there is no other
help or comfort, is also her.

iv
It is January, it's raining, this grey
ordinary day. My
daughter, I would like
your shirt to be just a shirt,
no charms or fables. But fables
and charms swarm here
in this January world,
entrenching us like snow, and few
are friendly to you; though
they are strong,
potent as viruses
or virginal angels dancing
on the heads of pins,
potent as the hearts
of whores torn out
by the roots because they were thought
to be solid gold, or heavy
as the imaginary
jewels they used to split
the heads of Jews for.

It may not be true
that one myth cancels another.
Nevertheless, in a corner
of the hem, where it will not be seen,
where you will inherit
it, I make this tiny stitch,
my private magic.

Margaret Atwood

v
The shirt is finished: red
with purple flowers and pearl
buttons. My daughter puts it on,

hugging the colour
which means nothing to her
except that it is warm
and bright. In her bare

feet she runs across the floor,
escaping from us, her new game,
waving her red arms

in delight, and the air
explodes with banners.

148

Contributors' Notes

Alba Ambert was born in San Juan, Puerto Rico. An award-winning novelist, essayist, short story writer and poet, she is a well-known advocate of bilingual education and has worked as a community activist and defender of Latino children's educational rights in the United States. She has also published several books for children. She is now Writer in Residence at Richmond, the American International University in London.

Sherry Ashworth lives in Manchester with a husband, two teenage daughters, and two cats. She gave up dieting while writing her first novel, *A Matter of Fat*, and now exists happily on chicken soup, Chardonnay and Uncle Joe's Mint Balls. She teaches English part-time and continues to write novels.

Margaret Atwood was born in Ottawa in 1939 and spent much of her early life in northern Ontario and Quebec. She is one of Canada's most distinguished writers and has published nine novels, five collections of short fiction and fourteen volumes of poetry. She has won numerous awards including the *Sunday Times* Author of the Year in 1993, the Arthur C Clarke Award for Science Fiction and the Governor-General's Award on two occasions. Three of her novels have also been shortlisted for the Booker Prize – *The Handmaid's Tale* (1986), *Cat's Eye* (1989) and *Alias Grace* (1996). She has been presented with twelve honorary degrees. Margaret

Atwood lives in Toronto with the writer Graeme Gibson and their daughter.

Susie Boyt is the author of two novels, *The Normal Man* and *The Characters of Love*. She lives in London with her husband Tom and is currently working on her third novel and a play.

Jean Buffong is a Grenadian living in London. Jean juggles a full-time job and community work with her successful career as a writer and her novels include *Jump up and Kiss Me*, *Snowflakes in the Sun* and the much acclaimed *Under the Silk Cotton Tree*. She has contributed to *A Stranger at My Table*, *A Glimpse of Green*, *Something to Savour* (all published by The Women's Press); *Flaming Work*, *Burning Images* and *Framing the Words*. She is the co-editor of the anthology *Just a Breath Away*, and wrote the Foreword to the British publication of *Sisterfire*, an anthology of African American women's writing. Jean is a member of the Caribbean Women Writers Alliance and the Chairperson of the Ananse Society.

Kate Cann lives in Twickenham with her husband, daughter, son and dog. She worked as an editor for many years before writing several books, including the bestselling *Diving In*, (Livewire, 1996), *In the Deep End* (Livewire, 1997) and *Sink or Swim* (Livewire, 1998).

Stevie Davies, who lives near Manchester, is a novelist and literary critic, an elected Fellow of the Royal Society of Literature. She has published numerous works of non-fiction including *Emily Brontë: Heretic* (The Women's Press, 1994) and her hugely successful book on women of the English Revolution, *Unbridled Spirits* (The Women's Press, 1998). She is also a distinguished writer of fiction whose novels include *Boy Blue* (The Women's Press, 1987) which won the Fawcett Book Prize; and *Closing the Book* (The Women's Press, 1994) which was on the longlist for the Booker Prize and the shortlist for the Fawcett Book Prize. Her next novel, *Impassioned Clay*, will be published by The Women's Press in 1999.

Catherine Temma Davidson has received numerous accolades for her poetry, including an award from the Academy of American Poets and the Dorothy Daniels Award from PEN. Her first novel, *The Priest Fainted*, was published by The Women's Press in 1998 to great critical acclaim. Catherine Temma Davidson teaches at Richmond, the American International University, and lives in London.

Sarah Dreher was born in 1937, in a small town in Pennsylvania. She gained an AB degree from Wellesley College, and an MS and Ph.D. in Clinical Psychology from Purdue University in Indiana. In 1965 she moved to Massachusetts and has been in private practice as a clinical psychologist there ever since. She began writing mysteries at the age of 40, as Christmas gifts for friends. She has published seven novels in the Stoner McTavish series, including *Stoner McTavish* (The Women's Press, 1996), and *Bad Company* (The Women's Press, 1996), and a book of plays. She has won several national and international playwriting contests.

Patricia Duncker was born in Jamaica and is now Senior Lecturer in the Department of English at the University of Wales, Aberystwyth, where she teaches writing, literary theory and nineteenth-century literature. Her critical work includes *Sisters and Strangers: An Introduction to Contemporary Feminist Fiction* (1992). She is the editor of *In and Out of Time: Lesbian Feminist Fiction* (1990), and co-editor, with Vicky Wilson, of *Cancer through the eyes of ten women* (1996) to which she is also a contributor. Her first novel, *Hallucinating Foucault* (1996) won the Dillons First Fiction Award and the McKitterick Prize and has been translated into several languages. Her most recent publication is a collection of short fiction, *Monsieur Shoushana's Lemon Trees* (1997).

Helen Dunmore is a poet, novelist, short-story writer and children's author. Her latest novel is *Your Blue-Eyed Boy* (1998), and a collection of short stories, *Love of Fat Men*, was published at the same time. She has won many awards for her work, including the inaugural Orange Prize for Fiction for *A Spell of Winter* (1996).

Catherine Dunne was born in Dublin in 1954. She read English and Spanish at Trinity College, Dublin, and went on to teach at Greendale Community School. She lives in Dublin with her husband and her son. Her first novel, *In the Beginning*, was published in 1997, and her second, *A Name for Himself*, in 1998. She is currently working on her third book.

Caryn Franklin. Ex fashion editor and co-editor of *I-D* magazine in the eighties, Caryn Franklin went on to present the BBC's Clothes Show for twelve years. She now presents BBC's Style Challenge. An accomplished director, she made her own reports from places as far afield as Bosnia in order to highlight refugees' need for clothing. She is also a writer, a lecturer and external assessor to a variety of fashion colleges. Caryn is a patron of the Eating Disorders Association and Co-Chairwoman of Fashion Targets Breast Cancer, and is currently working on her third book.

Janice Galloway has written four books: *The Trick is to Keep Breathing* and *Foreign Parts* (novels); and *Blood* and *Where You Find It* (short stories). Her awards include the American Academy of Arts and Letters E M Forster Award, the McVitie's Prize, and the MIND/Allan Lane Award. She has one son and lives in Glasgow.

Hiromi Goto was born in 1966 in Japan, and emigrated to Canada at the age of three with her family. After a short time on the West Coast, they moved to southern Alberta. Hiromi graduated with a BA degree in English from the University of Calgary in 1989. Her first novel, *Chorus of Mushrooms* (The Women's Press, 1997), won the Commonwealth Writers' Prize for Best First Book, Canada and the Caribbean Region, and was also the co-winner of the Canada–Japan Book Award in 1996. She lives in Calgary with her two children, is an active member of the Calgary Women of Color Collective; and is currently working on her next novel.

Sarah Harris was born in 1967. She graduated from the London School of Economics in 1988 and has worked as a press officer for the Liberal Democrats and as an assistant producer for BBC's Newsnight. Her first novel, *Wasting Time*, was published in 1998 and she is currently working on her second. Married, with one child, she lives in North London.

bell hooks is Distinguished Professor of English at City College of New York. She is renowned for her books on race and feminism. Her first memoir, *Bone Black: Memories of Girlhood*, was published by The Women's Press in 1997, and her second, *Wounds of Passion*, in 1998.

Manju Kak is the author of two books of fiction: *First Light in Colonelpura* and *Requiem for an Unsung Revolutionary*. She has written articles, essays and reviews for several newspapers and journals. She held the Charles Wallace Creative Writing Fellowship at the University of Stirling in 1995. Presently she works as a Consultant for the Indian Department of Culture in the field of heritage and conservation in the Himalayas, and political empowerment of women, on which she also currently holds a fellowship.

A L Kennedy has published three collections of short stories and two novels, all them winning prizes including the Somerset Maugham Award. She was listed among Granta's twenty Best of Young British Novelists and has written for the stage, film and television. A new novel *Everything You Need* will be published in Spring 1999.

Deborah Levy is the author of four novels: *Beautiful Mutants*, *Swallowing Geography*, *The Unloved*, and *Billy and Girl*. She is currently writing a work of non-fiction, *The Snowman*.

Carol Mara is an Australian writer. She has published a collection of short stories and her first novel, *Iron Cradles*, is to be published in February 1999.

Caeia March was born on the Isle of Man in 1946 and grew up in industrial South Yorkshire. She went to London University in 1964 and graduated in Social Sciences. She has published poetry, short stories and non-fiction articles, but is best known for her novels, all published by The Women's Press – *Three Ply Yarn* (1986), *The Hide and Seek Files* (1988), *Fire! Fire!* (1991), *Reflections* (1995) and *Between the Worlds* (1996). She is also the editor of a collection of women's writing on myalgic encephalomyelitis and chronic fatigue syndrome, *Knowing ME* (1998). She lives in Cornwall with her partner, Cheryl Straffon, and two cats.

Kate Mosse is a novelist and short-story writer and the author of two non-fiction books, *Becoming a Mother* and *The House: A Year in the Life of the Royal Opera House, Covent Garden*, which accompanied the award-winning BBC television series of the same name. Her début novel, *Eskimo Kissing*, was published to widespread critical acclaim in 1996. Her second novel, *Crucifix Lane* – a feminist thriller set in the future – was published in November 1998 and she is currently researching her third, which is set in thirteenth-century France. Kate Mosse is also a co-founder and the Honorary Director of the Orange Prize for Fiction and is a member of the Arts for Everyone panel of the Arts Council of England. She is Administrator of Chichester Festival Theatre, the first woman to hold the position. She lives with her partner and two children in West Sussex.

Freya North holds a Masters Degree in History of Art from the Courtauld Institute. She has worked for the National Arts Collections Fund as well as for a commercial sculpture garden and has freelanced as a picture researcher. *Polly*, published in November 1998, follows her first two highly acclaimed novels *Sally* and *Chloë*.

Joyce Carol Oates is the author of twenty-seven novels and numerous collections of short stories, poetry and plays. The winner of many prestigious literary awards, she is the Roger S Berlind Distinguished Professor of Humanities at Princeton University. She lives in Princeton, New Jersey.

Beverly Pagram was educated at Greycoats, Westminster, and the University of Western Australia. After a five-year stint as Women's Editor of Australia's largest Sunday paper she returned to England, where her journalistic career has included writing for many national newspapers and magazines. Her most recent book, *Heaven and Hearth* (The Women's Press, 1997), is a seasonal compendium of women's spiritual and domestic lore. Beverly now lives in Oxfordshire with her scriptwriter husband and two daughters.

Elisa Segrave was born in 1949 and taken to Spain aged six weeks. She was educated at a convent for six years. Her first book *The Diary of a Breast* was published in 1995 and her second *Ten Men* in 1997. She also writes short stories and articles. She is currently working on her third book, about her mother.

Bulbul Sharma is a painter and writer. She has published three collections of short stories – *My Sainted Aunts* (1992), *The Perfect Woman* (1994) and *Anger of the Aubergines* (1997). She has also written and illustrated a book on Indian birds for children. She works as an art teacher for disabled children.

Carol Shields's novels include *Larry's Party*, winner of the 1998 Orange Prize for Fiction; *The Stone Diaries* (1993), winner of the Pulitzer Prize and shortlisted for the Booker Prize; *The Republic of Love* (1992), *Happenstance* (1991) and *Mary Swann* (1990). *Various Miracles*, a collection of short stories, was published in 1994. Born and brought up in Chicago, Carol Shields has lived in Canada since 1957. She is the Chancellor of the University of Winnipeg.

Joan Smith is a novelist, essayist and journalist. She is the author of five novels, and two books of essays entitled *Misogynies* and *Different for Girls*. She has written weekly columns for the *Independent on Sunday* and her work appears regularly in the *Guardian*, the *Financial Times*, and *Tribune*. She lives in London.

Susan Stinson grew up in Colorado. Her fiction and poetry have appeared in several anthologies and magazines including *Sinister Wisdom* and *The Kenyon Review*. She is also the author of *Belly Songs: In Celebration of Fat Women*, and two novels – *Fat Girl Dances with Rocks* and *Martha Moody* (The Women's Press, 1996). She lives in Northampton, Massachusetts.

Andrea Stuart was born in the Caribbean and has lived briefly in the United States and Paris, as well as London. She has worked as a journalist, TV producer, and in publishing. She has contributed to a wide range of magazines from *Cosmopolitan* to the *New Statesman*. She works as a lecturer in Cultural Studies at Central St Martin's College of Art and Design in London. Her first book, *Showgirls*, was published in 1996 and she is currently working on a biography of the Empress Josephine.

Joanna Traynor was born in London and raised in the north of England. She has worked as a nurse, a sales manager and an IT consultant. Her first novel, *Sister Josephine*, won the Saga Prize in 1996, and her second novel, *Divine*, was published in 1998. She now lives in Devon.